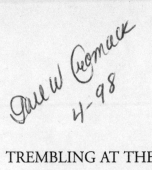

TREMBLING AT THE THRESHOLD
OF A BIBLICAL TEXT

Trembling at the Threshold of a Biblical Text

JAMES L. CRENSHAW

WILLIAM B. EERDMANS PUBLISHING COMPANY
GRAND RAPIDS, MICHIGAN

Copyright © 1994 by Wm. B. Eerdmans Publishing Co.
255 Jefferson Ave. S.E., Grand Rapids, Michigan 49503
All rights reserved

Printed in the United States of America

Library of Congress Cataloging-in-Publication Data

Crenshaw, James L.
Trembling at the threshold of a biblical text / James L. Crenshaw.
p.   cm.
Includes index.
ISBN 0-8028-0720-8 (pbk.)
1. Bible. O.T. — Sermons. 2. Sermons, American. 3. Christian life —
1960 — Meditations. 4. Prayers. I. Title.
BS1151.5.C74 1994
252 — dc20   94-5573
                                                  CIP

To Cynthia Tyler Crenshaw
A SCRIBE'S PRAYER

IF
I were the pen
In your hand
I would yield
To your touch
And pour myself out
That you might
Be manifest
To others.

IF
I were the ink
In your pen
I would take shape
On the page
As you breathe,
Dancing
Before your eyes
For eternity.

IF
I were a page
In your diary
I would drink
From your pen,
Absorb your thoughts,
And mirror
Your soul.

IF
I were the cover
Of your diary
I would shelter
Your passion
From prying eyes
And surround you
With tenderness.

JAMES L. CRENSHAW
23 DECEMBER 1989

Contents

Introduction

From the moment of birth to the instant that death snuffs out our existence, we are subject to space and time. These same two properties, temporality and spatiality, mark thresholds. We speak of standing at the threshold of a new era, the threshold occupying space in neither the past nor the future. Thresholds function as a barrier between inside and outside, thus separating those who dwell within a residence from persons outside it. Ancient Canaanites, among others, associated thresholds with demons, who were thought to lurk underneath and to attack hapless persons disturbing their rest. Apprehension over falling into the grasp of powerful forces thus gave rise to the ritual practice of leaping over thresholds, presumably as a precaution against arousing sleeping demons. The modern groom who carries a bride across the threshold of their new dwelling bears witness to the tenacity of ancient popular beliefs, which survive long after the basis for such thinking crumbles.

Anyone who endeavors to understand a biblical text encounters a threshold under which lurk untold "demons." Careless interpreters of the past, as well as all too many modern ones, have trod loosely over thresholds, unleashing nightmarish evil. The text, although written by men and women in their own language, has been granted a privileged position above every other human production. This canonizing of a text by and for a religious community was attributed to divine inspiration. Naturally, such a bold claim cannot be corroborated, for the affirmation falls within the domain of faith. Even if the text were to make the claim on its own behalf, which it does not do, the assertion of divine inspiration cannot be self-validating. Those Christians who readily dismiss similar claims in non-Christian sacred texts merely illustrate the blindness that strikes so many religious people who are unaware of their plight.

I have no doubt about the human quality of the text, which confronts me at every reading. Indeed, I must spend countless hours combating the demons released on an unsuspecting society. The biblical text has been used to sanction slavery; the suppression of women; the burning of numerous women suspected of being witches; the murder of heretics and other individuals pejoratively labeled "the heathen"; the forced baptism of unbelievers and the imperialization of cultures under the dual flags of Christianity and a Western state; the perverted sense of the body that produced extreme asceticism and created an exaggerated enslavement to sex; the heavy guilt imposed on persons who, for whatever reason, departed from the proclaimed sexual norm; the jingoism and narrow fundamentalism that damns others who read texts differently; the refusal to endorse scientific fact and to benefit from its medicinal cures. The list could go on indefinitely, for the demons replicate themselves, like apocalyptic predictions that calculate the times anew with every failed forecast of the end.

The text possesses other human qualities for which I sense no need to apologize. Rare individuals search within themselves to discover the essence of creaturehood. They explore the mystery of suffering, the power of religious memory, the tyranny of time, the sense of wonder, the exhilaration of eros, the fidelity of love, the obligation of belonging, the divine pathos. In the broken testimony of countless believers from previous ages, I see myself and sometimes also those persons who have crossed my path over the years. The biblical witness bears the imprint of limited intellect, moral blind spots, and cultural biases, but so do my own ventures into making sense of the human condition. My encounter with the biblical text constitutes a dialogue in which deep cries out to deep, eventuating in a virtual encounter with silence. My hope is that the silencing is mutual, the text at times silencing those voices in me that ring hollow, and my own voice occasionally drowning out ancient cacophony.

But not always, for noisy gongs best describe the character of some experiences.

Although existential angst unites me with an ancient text, I am separated from that record by a linguistic and cultural barrier. The writers of the Bible thought in languages foreign to me, however well I may have learned to read them. Hebrew, Aramaic, and Greek differ among themselves, and as a totality they differ greatly from English. Crossing the threshold from one to the other language is fraught with difficulty. To translate literally, and thus to lie, or to paraphrase, and in doing so, to blaspheme — that dilemma faces anyone attempting the translator's turn. In translating an ancient text, I journey from one country to another, crossing the dangerous threshold separating me from the land I wish to visit. In due time I retrace my steps for the purpose of familiarizing readers with terrain they have never trod. When translating a text, I escort readers on a treacherous journey along precipitous mountain trails, through dense jungles, into sharp ravines, and through pleasant valleys. Because every act of translation inevitably involves an interpretive decision, I enter into the broader task of interpretation even while searching for the original meaning of a text.

Crossing the threshold brings me into immediate contact with an alien culture, for which my linguistic and cultural system frequently has no equivalents. Modes of subsistence, family structures, societal organizations, transmission of news, means of travel, educational settings — these and much more separate the two cultures, then and now. Interpreting ancient texts requires me to take up residence in a foreign country and to adopt its ways, abandoning values and presuppositions acquired in an altogether different land. Communicating the newly adopted worldview, once I have returned to more familiar territory, is no small task. In this significant endeavor, analogy plays a dominant role. Within the text from the past, I search for analogies that illustrate the functioning of moral discourse, the posing of choices, the analysis of hidden meanings in ordinary events.

Every text carries within its spaces multiple meanings, the polyvalency of speech itself. Contemporary literary theorists echo the voice of early midrashists and ecclesiastical theologians — texts may rightly be understood in several different ways. Our decision to concentrate on the author, or the text, or the reader affects the results of inquiry into the sense of a literary unit. The biblical text is indeed "fraught with background," to use the language of Erich Auerbach, who says that its rich allusive quality forces interpreters to supply the missing ingredients. Passive reading thus has no place in scriptural interpretation; the text calls for active participation at every juncture. Openness characterizes the act of reading precisely because that rich potential marks the ancient text. Meanings deconstruct at every level, forcing readers to begin the interpretive process anew. Finite creatures inevitably arrive at historically contingent understandings of reality; our relentless quest for the absolute is destined to be frustrated forever.

Why then do I tremble at the threshold of a biblical text? Should I not derive a measure of comfort from the knowledge that rich diversity characterizes all texts, increasing the likelihood that my understanding of their meaning may actually ring true? I use the category of dread for two reasons. First, the religious community that nurtured me has vested divine authority in the text, and whether Transcendence actually had anything to do with its composition or not, we have chosen to submit our will to the Hidden One whom our ancestors discerned behind the scenes played out in Judean hills. I freely choose to join them in listening for an authentic voice, human or divine, that enriches life in community. I tremble under the weight of uttering a faithful word, one that does justice to the sacred text and also to the human situation. One source of my anxiety, then, derives from my sense that I have been entrusted with a weighty message, the burden of which is lessened little by the extent of professional competence I may have obtained along the way. In the pulpit, as well as in classrooms where theological students seek guidance for their ministry, I struggle to render faithful witness to ancestral testimony.

The second reason for my trembling at the threshold of a biblical text rests in my own skeptical disposition, a critical attitude that characterizes everything I do. I doubt precisely because of an inner vision, a perceived disparity between the world of my experience and the one I envision for humankind. Reason forces me to concede that the evidence supporting age-old claims is meager, whereas staggering arguments can easily be mustered against them. I wish, therefore, to be faithful to the present community, religious or otherwise, and I do not know the extent to which my experience coincides with that of others. With one foot firmly planted in the modern age and the other tentatively feeling for a toehold in the biblical period, I risk the fury of Legion, the demons lurking beneath the threshold. Would that, like King Solomon of later legend, I could gather my bride, Wisdom, in my arms and leap over the threshold into that strange world of full knowledge.

My courtship of Wisdom has produced amorous moments but hardly a marriage ensuing in complete knowledge. Hence I shall continue my passionate pursuit, hoping to discover appropriate ways to link two distinct worlds. By constructing a window so that modern readers can peer into remote spaces peopled by Israelites and early Christians, and by fashioning a mirror in which my contemporaries can examine themselves in the light of what they learn from looking through the windowpanes, I hope to highlight the saving virtue of the biblical text: its capacity for self-criticism. If I dare to question what some readers consider sacrosanct, warrant for such criticism rests in the remarkable willingness of some ancient religious thinkers to question what they understood to be divine conduct. Still, their remonstrations with Deity sprang from profound faith and gave voice to a decision to cling to the living God even when nothing seemed to justify such faithfulness. That situation is exactly the one in which I find myself — trembling because of the silence of eternity and the anticipation of hearing the clamor from the past.

*　　　*　　　*

I began teaching the Bible in the fall semester of 1964, offering courses in both Old Testament and New Testament until January of 1970. From that wintry day until now, my attention has been focused entirely on the Old Testament and its Near Eastern setting. During the last twenty-three years I have taught students in two highly regarded Divinity Schools, Vanderbilt (1970-1987) and Duke (1987-), as well as undergraduates and students in M.A. and Ph.D. programs. I have also preached occasional sermons in Benton Chapel at Vanderbilt and in York Chapel at Duke. These rare appearances in the pulpit during my teaching career gave me the opportunity to move from text to sermon, from "what the text meant to what it means." Divinity students constantly express a need for guidance in making this epochal leap in interpretation. They frequently complain that the Divinity classroom prepares them well for the exegetical task but poorly for the move from text to sermon. The publication of the sermons in this book represents my response to this plea for instruction.

These brief sermons mark the religious landscape of one who has been fortunate beyond description, for I have had esteemed colleagues from whom I learned daily. Some of them were my mentors at Vanderbilt in earlier years; they and others encouraged me to cultivate a critical mind, and they always respected opinions at variance with their own, even when expressed in pulpits. Many of my teachers and colleagues taught me by example, for their sermons in Benton Chapel stirred my soul at the same time they stretched my mind. I shall never forget specific sermons by Lee Keck, Lou Silberman, Gordon Kaufman, Langdon Gilkey, Kelly Miller Smith, Walter Harrelson, and Jack Forstman, to name only a few. Kaufman's questioning the motives for the Easter faith (which sent shock waves through the student body), Smith's skill at storytelling, Gilkey's lively use of dialogic discourse, Forstman's effective exploration of German novels to question contemporary religious beliefs, Silberman's silver-tongued oratory in the service of faithful witness, Harrelson's willingness to affirm God's existence despite cogent arguments to the contrary, Keck's close reading of biblical texts — all have profoundly influenced my own preaching. In my sermons I have tried to continue the tradition that these teachers and colleagues themselves began at Vanderbilt.

Like my critical research in Hebrew Bible, these sermons are allusive and brief. Some may say too brief. But I have pointedly made an effort to strip away all nonessentials, in the confidence that careful readers will find enough to ponder for countless hours. I have tried not to insult readers' intelligence, for I trust them to develop my ideas in ways that correspond to their own particular religious beliefs and circumstances. Indeed, many readers will recognize faint signs that I have traveled numerous side paths before returning to the main trail, having become convinced that the detour would neither edify readers nor clarify the text being discussed.

From time to time I have been asked to pray at university functions, and I have always done so with considerable trepidation. Occasionally, I have shared some of these prayers with students in a class on biblical prayer that I have taught for several years. My primary aim in this class has been to explore the vexing issue of intercessory prayer: does prayer change things, or is its effect limited to people, and hence mainly cathartic? My students have urged me to publish these prayers, and I have yielded to their promptings, offering some of the prayers for broader circulation. If these outpourings of my spirit give the impression of a cosmic scream, they are certainly that. Nevertheless, I believe they also convey my great sense of awe and gratitude in the presence of the gift of life and its silent Source. That feeling also underlies the sermons and meditations here offered to the reading public for the first time.

In preparing this manuscript for publication, I have been greatly assisted by the exceptional typing skills of Anita Gail Chappell and Sarah S. Freedman. Their professional manner and generous spirit have made working with them a pleasure. Translations of biblical texts are my own, with occasional exceptions, where I use the Revised Standard Version.

SERMONS

A Stairway to Heaven

Genesis 11:1-9

The human imagination has always flirted with the possibility of building a ladder that joins heaven to earth, of bringing the two realms together so that one could travel back and forth at will. That impossible dream has expressed itself in various ways, but realism has always forced an admission that anyone who dared ascend that stairway must be really special.

The Bible often links heaven and earth in this fashion. Stories tell of Enoch of old, who walks with God, and eventually the two simply walk hand in hand into the clouds of glory. Elijah's departure from this world is much more dramatic. The fearless prophet climbs aboard God's chariot of fire and rides off into the sunset. Jesus, too, leaves earth in glorious fashion, floating along on billowy clouds.

Now we all know that such things do not happen in real life, at least for ordinary people. Still, we persist in dreaming the impossible dream. To reach the unreachable star — that is our task. Like Jacob, we dream of angels ascending and descending a ladder that God has dropped from heaven, and we long, like Peter of old, to build a tent and dwell with God on his holy mountain.

If we cannot reach heaven, since we are flesh and blood, perhaps we can scale the heights with our thoughts. Believing this, we recognize certain persons as mediators of the two worlds, and give credence to a Bible that claims to be the product of such two-way communication. Prophets and poets, we think, heard the heavenly voice that remains concealed from us, while priestly lawgivers stood in a special relationship with the hidden realm. Eventually we even grant the possibility that God's wisdom descended to earth, and we go on from there to assert that the living God has for a time taken on the form of flesh and blood.

Once again, haunting realism forces us to concede that all claims of hearing special voices from on high may arise from sick minds. If this is the case today, we ask, why hasn't it always been the same? Thus we are forced to conclude that a huge question mark hangs over stories about human beings who "actually" climbed that ladder as well as about those who took a mental journey from earth to heaven.

Against every reason, your presence here this morning grows out of profound conviction that the two realms can touch one another. Nothing else adequately explains your readiness to come to this place again and again, hoping for a miracle. You did not come here to hear a brilliant sermon, to listen to uplifting music, to be entertained, or to greet a friend after the service. No, a hundred times no. You came here because you believe in the possibility of linking your life with God, who gave you life in the beginning. You have come because your hearts are restless until they find rest in God. You — yes, we — have come because we desire above everything else to encounter the living God, and we dare to expose our lives to the searching gaze of the eternal Judge.

I cannot guarantee that we shall meet God here this morning. In all honesty, I have to concede the possibility that you may go home without finding the rest that only God can give. Furthermore, I have to grant the possibility that we are all deceiving ourselves in even hoping that God may meet us in worship. All I can promise is that we live in hope. If we do experience a miracle of faith, and God's hand reaches down and touches ours the way a parent lovingly takes hold of a child's hand in the terrifying dark, then the initiative will come from above. God alone can span the gulf between heaven and earth, for as Jeremiah realized, the One we worship is both a God far off and one most near.

The Bible purports to be a record of decisive moments when the silence of eternity was broken, when eternity entered time. Our text offers one of those rare moments when human pride sought to lay violent hands on God and to enslave Deity for selfish desires. Let us listen for God's voice in this old story, one with which you may be vaguely familiar. For background, I wish only to point out that it contains a memory of a Babylonian ziggurat, a temple tower, and that the writer thinks such a building illustrates the human desire to link heaven and earth. The setting into which the narrator placed the story is important. It follows hard upon the account of the devastating flood. In my analysis of the story, I wish to lift out three ideas and to comment upon their implications: the people had few words, they hoped to make a name for themselves, and God sent confusion upon them.

Let us first reflect on the limited vocabulary of the ancient construction workers. The Bible states that they had one language and few words. In so short a narrative, the people use the same words twice: "Come, let us . . ." In an exquisite bit of irony, God uses the same expression: "Come, let us go down." Apparently, God adapts to their limited vocabulary and communicates far more than parsimonious speech normally does.

In some ways I envy these ancient peoples. They had few words, so we can assume that they knew the joys of silence. I recently came across a Yiddish proverb that struck me as quite profound: "Beautiful silence is better than fine speech." Biblical proverbs, too, knew the beauty of proper silence, and in Egypt the wise person was known as the silent one. Perhaps one of the reasons I like Ecclesiastes so much is that he knew there was a time for silence. Even the prophets recognized that certain times demanded silence: "The Lord is in his holy temple. Let all the earth keep silence before him." And at the very end of the Bible, the book of Revelation speaks of silence in heaven for a definite period of time. How else could one respond to divine presence?

The Bible also knew the sanctity of words. Jesus counseled his disciples to let their yes and no be sufficient, and warned against using empty repetitions in prayer. Jewish rabbis even went so far as to prohibit the use of numerous adjectives in praising God, the guardian of truth.

Today we have lost the sanctity of words, and we bombard

others with words from morning to night. Our story implies that, possessing few words, these people who built a tower to heaven used their words loosely. They spoke without realizing the consequences of their few words. Are we any different?

Second, the people desired to make a name for themselves. Overcome by blind ambition, they hoped to avoid dispersion. But dispersing was exactly what God had ordered them to do, to scatter out and fill the far reaches of the earth. So they defied their Creator and chose to play God. If they could only build a stairway to heaven, they could escape the next flood sent by an angry deity. Then they could live as they pleased, fearing nothing. So they envisioned an escape route. Defiant pride in the service of immortality — that is what the story illustrates. These people hoped to be God by forcing the true God to play servant to their slightest whim. Ready access to God at all times meant that. The irony of the text is that they are not even named. Who were these people who wished to make a name for themselves? Further irony occurs when this story is immediately followed by a genealogy of Shem, whose name means "name."

Surely, we can identify with these people. Fearing extinction, we freeze our bodies and build storm shelters and space shuttles. Who among us does not breathe the air of ambition, has not drunk the heady wine of desire to achieve something truly extraordinary — even if only in our secret daydreams? We kill ourselves making bricks, meeting deadlines, and for what purpose? In the end, God will come down, and our puny anthills will be washed away with the next light sprinkle.

The story is inherently funny. We envision God peering down from heaven, or up, or whatever, and squinting divine eyes in a vain effort to catch a glimpse of the majestic tower that was supposed to reach heaven. To see it, God had to go down. What a commentary on human achievement that stands in the shadow of God's overwhelming statement about human possibility: "Nothing is impossible for them!"

To be sure, our individual towers may be worthy goals. We may build towers to heaven by our good works and piety, but they, too, will crumble in ruins. Try as we may, we cannot control our future. God will see to that.

My third comment concerns God's response: "Let us go down and confuse their speech." Now that is a surprising way to describe God's action. Or is it? Doesn't God always introduce confusion into human lives? How neatly we could live if the God question had no claim upon our being. How tidy our lives could be. Our epitaphs would read "born, suffered, died." No illusions of glorious future, no belief that destiny beckons to nobler action — how simple life would be if there were no God.

Yes, God confuses our minds on every hand. God challenges every answer, deepens every mystery, introduces wonder in all of life. When we think we have some grasp on reality, Jesus forces us to think again. How confusing: "I came to bring a sword, to set father against son and mother against daughter." The God who bestows life takes it back again, and the One who prohibits murder demands that Abraham offer his own beloved son and, in the end, slays an only son on the Cross. The balm of Gilead breaks human hearts too. What a strange God we serve. Such coming down is too much for us, and we confess that we cannot enslave God even with our ideas about deity. God remains sovereign Lord, and we object mightily. But what glorious confusion this brings. In the story, God uses human pride to accomplish the divine will, for the people now scatter because they cannot communicate with one another.

What do we do in the face of such mystery? Like the disciples whom Jesus joined on the road to Emmaus, we express our utter confusion just when God is supremely near: "We had hoped it would have been he who would redeem Israel. . . . Yet our hearts burned within us while he talked with us on the way." Make no mistake about it. God's entrance into our lives is no laughing matter. In Jewish tradition, three men managed to scale that ladder to heaven and gazed upon God's face. One died, another went mad, and the third lived to tell about it. Confronting ultimate mystery, let us be silent and marvel at the confusion God brings. Perhaps then we can bow down and worship before the mystery that lets itself be glimpsed from afar. Then and only then can we experience the power of Pentecost that turned this story upside down.

You Shall Become Like God

Genesis 3

The story of open revolt in paradise conceals a hidden impulse within the human breast: to become like God. Scripture elsewhere encourages this desire, urging men and women to imitate God, being holy as God is holy. A constant source of inspiration, this wish to be like God generates conduct of a saintly character and promotes ethical behavior despite great personal cost to the individual. At the same time, the impulse to imitate God lures us toward positions of increasing power, status, and privilege. On the one hand, it fosters unselfish actions for the benefit of others; on the other hand, the hidden impulse generates exclusive concern for one's self at any price. Furthermore, even its admirable features elicit inner tension, inasmuch as we cannot really be like God, however much we try. Although I may see and approve what is good, in actual practice I frequently follow its opposite. That is Paul's well-known confession, replicated in almost the exact words by contemporaries of his, the poet Ovid and the philosopher Epictetus.

Traditionally, three explanations for human proclivity to sin have been suggested. The tragic response places all blame on the gods, who for no good reason except divine prerogative strike human victims with moral blindness. The dualistic answer likewise accuses the gods, who are locked in eternal conflict with opposing forces, with human beings caught up in the consequences of such a struggle, the body opting for one side and the soul for the other side. The Adamic response lays the responsibility for a fall on human shoulders, although conceding that God is not wholly free from blame. After

all, God created the occasion for the temptation, the beguiling
pent. Nevertheless, the biblical story understands the fall as a per
act of rebellion, one resulting in both guilt and punishment.
viewed here as the creature's rejection of limits, an act that per
human relationships and introduces an existential exploration
concept of death.

The story wrestles with the presence of various enigmas
a good creation. Why is there death, pain at the inception
toil, enmity, subjection, sexual desire? Genesis 3 concerns the tv
zone before time, the juncture of beginning and non-existen
literary craft the author fashions linkages with the preceding na
about creation. These connections include the reference to t
in the middle of the garden, the divine prohibition against ea
fruit, and the clever pun between the lovers' nakedness a
beguiling power of the serpent. The title of this sermon derive
the serpent's motto: God knows that when you eat the fruit or the
tree, you will become like God.

The structure of the story consists of dialogue, drama, dialogue,
drama. The dialogue begins on the subhuman level and ends with
God delivering a monologue and acting alone.

The initial dialogue between serpent and woman plants a seed
of doubt in her mind. Beginning with a distortion of the truth that
launches an attack on God's benevolence, the serpent thus pretends
to give woman the advantage. "Has God really said, 'You shall not
eat of any tree in the garden'?" In other words, "God is actually a
tyrant, withholding good things from your enjoyment." Naturally,
the question arises whenever one thinks of human limits. What
purpose do they serve? Are restrictions merely God's means of stifling
human initiative? Perhaps, too, ancient notions of woman's vulnerability evoke the present form of the story, for Greek legend attributed evil to the curiosity of a woman, Pandora. Worse still, it
blamed this unfortunate woman for suppressing all hope of deliverance from this strife-torn world.

Eve's defense of God strikes readers as somewhat overzealous.
Indeed, she even assumes the role of God, creating a new articulation
of the prohibition, one significantly different from the original

Faithful Fool
Tenderloin Street Ministr

REV. KAY JORGENSEN
SR. CARMEN BARSODY, OSF
370 Turk Street, Suite 371
San Francisco, CA 94121
Carmen's pager: 415.270.065
Kay's pager: 415.560.9698
Fax: 415.776.4400
e-mail: carmenb@value.net

decree. "We may eat of any tree in the garden — any, that is, except the one in the middle, and we must not "touch that one, or we will die." God had said nothing about touching the fruit. The woman has been considering the forbidden fruit and has protected herself by strengthening the divine prohibition. In the words of later rabbis, she erected a fence around the Torah.

The plot contains inherent flaws at two points. A single tree gives way to two trees: a tree the fruits of which produce knowledge, and another tree that bestows life on those who eat its fruit, An ancient parallel from the Gilgamesh Epic throws fresh light on the erotic background of the phrase "knowing good and evil," a sense virtually erased from the biblical story. The Gilgamesh Epic also features the tree of life and its theft by a serpent. The flaws — one tree or two and sexual knowledge or lack of it — have been covered over with consummate skill

The initial dialogue concludes with an assertive, authoritative serpent, one no longer content to pretend weakness. "You will not die," the serpent insists, which also confirms that God is a tyrant. "Obviously, God has tasted the fruit and acquired the knowledge it grants. God therefore knows that your eyes will also be opened if you eat."

A human drama unfolds as a consequence of this intriguing dialogue. The woman examines the fruit more closely, asking all the right questions. Her examination concluded, she confirms that the fruit is pleasing sensually, aesthetically, and rationally. What more could anyone ask? The fruit belongs to the categories of the desirable, the beautiful, and the intellectual. In essence, Eve attempts to define her own limits and to live from her own resources. That is precisely what makes the food so appealing.

We see immediately that sin is a social phenomenon. The sinner desires company, for the fun increases when one can share the rebellion with others. Having eaten of the fruit, the woman gives some to her husband, who was standing there the whole time but who lacked initiative or curiosity. The man eats, whether from sympathy or desire. Eve's generosity has now resulted in personal defiance. Another thing comes from this joint feast, a potentially positive self-awareness — one that in its present guise produces a sense of

shame. The sinning pair begin to concentrate on their own nakedness; self-centered thinking proves that clothes are for the sinful. The
first cover-up addresses this perceived offense. The seed of doubt has
sprouted into open revolt.

Shame's companion, fear, also enters the story. The sound of
the approaching Deity brings terror, although until now it merely
signaled imminent walks in the garden with the Creator. At this
important juncture, dialogue returns, ending in a curse. This time
the dialogue occurs on a suprahuman level. Unable to locate the
couple as they cower amidst the trees of the garden, the Lord God
addresses the man with the terrifying summons "Where are you?"
His response exposes open rebellion, albeit unintentionally. "I heard
you approaching and hid to conceal the fact that I was naked." So
much for the attempt to pull the wool over God's eyes. The mere
sound of divine footfalls sufficed to demolish every vestige of Ti-
tanism on the man's part.

What follows constitutes a dreadful inquisition. The man's
defenses fall in rapid succession as God asks one question after
another. "Who told you about your naked state?" "Have you eaten
from the forbidden fruit?" The man's excuse indicates that passing
the buck has a long history. "The woman you gave me is responsible."
Note the real culprit — God — in this formulation of the situation.
Implicit is the divine initiative in overcoming human loneliness, an
initiative that the rebel now finds unwelcome. He has earlier greeted
it with ecstatic eroticism. Now for the first time the Lord addresses
the woman, who needs only to blame the serpent, for God was surely
aware who placed it in the garden. Having no one to blame, the
serpent must endure a divine curse. This rebuke follows a reverse
sequence from the divine interrogation: first the serpent, then the
woman, and finally the man. In the punishment expressed here, we
see the early effort to explain some of life's enigmas. Serpents crawl
as punishment, and human beings despise them with reason. Women
give birth in pain and even must endure dominance by men, who
find nature wholly uncooperative in their quest for livelihood. Now
we hear the awful sentence that assures a short life to open revolt:
"You are dust, and to dust you will return." In the face of this dreadful

prospect, the man issues a final defiant assertion of egocentricity: he names his wife, Eve, "the mother of all living." The fruit of defiance has ripened.

Drama returns for one final act. God has compassion on the rebellious couple, fashioning clothes for them from the hides of animals. The couple's sin has already brought a rupture in relationships between them and nature. Now it extends that rupture to the animal realm, for God determines that shielding human shame is more important than the life of an animal. Furthermore, in allowing the sinners to live, God has confirmed the serpent's initial assertion. They did not die the day they tasted the fruit.

The closing scene finds God acting to prevent perpetual rebellion. The dualistic option simply held no appeal for this narrator. Conceding that the possibility of even more successful rebellion exists, God banishes the couple from the garden. They have become like God, living out of their own resources, making their own rules, setting their own limits. Lest they eat of the tree of life and live forever in a rebellious state, God appoints guardians at the entrance to the garden. With the mention of cherubim and a flaming sword, the story suddenly drifts off into the mythic past. Astonishingly, the Lord breaks off speaking in mid-sentence.

The story closes in profound sadness. Its message affirms that we do evil even when our sights are on target. The wish to become like God conceals our refusal to accept what we all are: creatures whose days are numbered. The wonder is that the story faces that bleak prospect and still proclaims a compassionate Lord who graciously turns to us sinners and covers our exposed selves even when holding us responsible for the consequences of our wrongdoing. The author of the Pauline hymn in Philippians 2 understood the dangers residing in the desire to be like God. That is why the hymn extols Jesus as one who did not grasp after equality with God but emptied himself, becoming a servant and, in the end, submitting to the Cross.

The Test of True Wisdom

Job 28:20-28; James 3:13-18

The practical application of human wisdom staggers the imagination. The poet pauses within the faltering debate between Job and his three friends, pondering humankind's amazing success at exploring the innermost recesses of the earth in search of precious ore. Nothing seems hidden from such persistent pursuit, and yet the most valued thing of all remains a dark secret about which rumors circulate among dubious, mythic creatures, Death and Abaddon, while God alone has access to true wisdom.

We can share the ancient poet's awe before early achievements of putting knowledge to work for useful ends. When groups came together for common cause, they needed a means of keeping records, so they developed a system of writing and eventually devised an alphabet. Wishing to assure a reliable source of food, they came up with an intricate system of terraces on the hills and irrigation canals in the plains. To provide water during periods of drought, they dug deep cisterns and chiseled underground tunnels through solid rock. For protection from enemies, they constructed thick walls and fashioned chariots and crossbows. Hoping to gain life in the next world, they built pyramids that remain sources of wonder to this day.

Modern accomplishments rival earlier ones. We are obsessed with speed, a striving to overcome time itself: the French Concorde, spaceships, instant fax communications, television images, computers for processing information. Health concerns also figure prominently in our application of knowledge for practical purposes. We split the atom in search of energy, build a model of DNA, discover penicillin and wonder drugs of all kinds. Ancient surgical procedures, however remarkable, are dwarfed by the routine nature of our transplants, laser surgery, and so much more.

Still, the sense of awe lingers. A month ago I stood in a hospital by my brother's side as the family gathered moments before he was to have a triple bypass operation to receive a new heart valve and, as things turned out, to have another valve repaired. Turning to the theologian in the family, he asked me to pray. Here was a time for me to say something profound; after all, I had studied theology most of my life. What did I say to God? Only this: "Our family has trusted you for nearly sixty years, and we are not going to stop now. Jerry's life is in your hands and in those of his surgeons. We want nothing more. Amen." Last Sunday Jerry and I talked for a long time about his walks in the woods with his grandson, whom he teaches the wonders of God's creation: the species of birds, the kinds of trees, the behavior of deer and foxes they encounter, and so forth. Who am I to belittle the use of knowledge for a better life?

Yet a cloud hovers over *our* knowledge, as one hovered over the reflections of the poet responsible for Job 28. Competing knowledge seems to require humility, hence pointing to relative truths. Postmodernism reminds us that every hypothesis bears the marks of cultural bias, historical accident, and linguistic arbitrariness. Our striving for objectivity, a heritage of the Enlightenment, is fraught with difficulty, for none of us can transcend time. We are products of our experience, and what we see comes to us through filters. To claim that we possess absolute truth constitutes the height of arrogance.

Thus we return to Job, who thought he had arrived at one incontrovertible fact: God owed him better things than he was experiencing. Such presumption is brilliantly attacked by the Yiddish author I. L. Peretz in a satirical story based on the book of Job and entitled *Bontshe the Silent*. This super-Job is bloodied from head to toe by life's vicissitudes, yet he refuses to lift his eyes to heaven in protest or to speak one word against humanity or God. Heaven trembles lest he make a claim on God, until his death brings rest on earth and in heaven. His trial before entering heaven's gates is thought to be a mere formality, and the Prosecuting Attorney wisely decides, like Bontshe, to be silent. God's messengers then bring a golden crown to Bontshe and offer him anything he wants: "Take whatever you want. Everything is yours." For the first time Bontshe raises his eyes, then wearily drops them. "Are you sure?" he asks. "Absolutely," the Presiding Judge affirms. After another questioning and repeated assurance, Bontshe answers, "Gee, if you mean it, what I'd really like is, each and every morning, a hot roll with fresh butter!" Judges and angels lower their heads in shame; the Prosecutor bursts out laughing. He has won. Bontshe is so simple that he values nothing except food for the stomach. In Peretz's view, docility is no virtue. Gustavo Gutiérrez's analysis of the book of Job from the perspective of poor persons who long for a fair distribution of wealth reveals a weakness in Peretz's interpretation and reminds us once more of historically conditioned readings.

Does any kind of knowledge ever transcend these limitations? The "Strawy Epistle" points to heavenly wisdom, by which it seems to mean knowledge that produces virtue. James stands in a worthy tradition reaching back into the earliest texts from ancient Egypt. In these instructions, knowledge must be embodied if it hopes to attain the elevated status of wisdom. This embodiment manifests itself in four cardinal virtues: eloquence, timing, restraint, and humility. Eloquence that persuades others to walk the path of life; timing that discerns the right moment for speech and for silence; restraint that holds passions in check — the appetites for food and sex, envy of others; and humility, a modesty borne in recognition of one's true ignorance before ultimate mystery. James would, I believe, applaud this understanding of embodiment.

Still, James introduces a new dimension into wisdom thinking: the contrast between heavenly and earthly knowledge. To be sure, the notion of personified wisdom in Proverbs, Sirach, and Wisdom of Solomon functions as a bridge between God's supreme wisdom and human insights, but this concept is different from the ideas James puts forth. For him, human wisdom issues from ambition and jealousy. Here he agrees with my favorite biblical author, Ecclesiastes, who thinks envy spurs us on to greater heights in a futile chase after meaning. In one respect James departs radically from Ecclesiastes, disallowing any space for doubt, Ecclesiastes' hallmark.

The metaphor about sowing a harvest of righteousness aligns James's teaching with that of Jesus, whose beatitude about peacemakers must surely underlie the curious image. Those of us who love to work in the garden quickly chide the author for mis-speaking: one sows seeds and anticipates the harvest; one does not sow a harvest. Furthermore, preparing soil for sowing seeds is a violent procedure, as those valuable earthworms in my garden can readily attest. We may cringe at James's imagery, but we certainly agree with his emphasis on a bountiful harvest of character as the result of heavenly wisdom.

One of my favorite texts from Jeremiah provides fresh com-mentary on what James wishes to say: "Let not the wise boast of wisdom, nor the rich of wealth, nor the mighty of strength, but that they know one who practices loving kindness, right dealing, and the enabling of the deserving in the land. In these things I delight, I the Lord." Here the prophet dismisses every cause for boasting and holds up the famous concepts of *hesed, mishpat,* and *s^edaqah.* Our praise thus finds its object in the Lord and in the fruits of divine wisdom.

The Epistle of James serves as a powerful reminder that Scrip-ture challenges our understandings of reality. While we daily sit in judgment on Scripture, it also does some judging. What more suit-able text could we find than this one to address a scholarly commu-nity? Ambition sets us apart, drives our waking moments, and lures us to ever-new hypotheses. Perhaps a bit of jealousy also takes resi-dence within us, despite our efforts to drive it away. To all of us James addresses a challenge: show me your wisdom by works worthy of God. Our way is to demonstrate wisdom by writing another book or by acing an exam, each laudable in itself, but the more enduring fruit of wisdom is embodied knowledge in which we become peacemakers.

In another short story, Peretz writes about the devout Rebbe of Nemirov, who always disappeared during the time of penitential prayers between New Year's and the Day of Atonement. Tradition arose that he ascended to heaven at this time each year to intercede for his people. One day a skeptic disguised himself and followed the Rebbe from a distance. Dressed as a humble peasant, the Rebbe was taking firewood to a poor sick woman. From that day forward when the people talked about the Rebbe's absence each year just before Yom Kippur and conjectured that he had gone up to heaven to intercede for them, the former skeptic would add these words: "If not still higher!"

Yes, our engineering skill is little short of mind-boggling, and the Yahwist's optimism seems appropriate: "There is nothing they can't do." Still, the potential for harm is boundless also, as James recognized. Perhaps we, too, can follow in the steps of the Rebbe of Nemirov and go still higher. Better yet, we can follow the Teacher of Nazareth and the One he proclaimed, manifesting our wisdom in loving deeds that establish peace. In these alone the One who is the Source of all knowledge takes pleasure.

Timing Is Everything

Haggai 2:1-9; 2 Thessalonians 1:5-10

Timing is everything — ask any athlete, lover, or public speaker. A split second too soon, and the ball veers off course, the beloved freezes, the joke malfunctions; but at the correct moment a stroke propels the ball into the stands, a loving touch evokes one in kind, and a word brings joy.

The texts for this morning raise the question of timing with absolute urgency, for they give voice to the age-old tendency to expect something desirable momentarily. These prophetic witnesses echo the child's anticipation that journey's end is just beyond the next curve, and in doing so they revitalize hope. In a little while the Lord will shake heaven and earth, sea and dry land, as one panning for gold shakes a sieve, and the nations' wealth will fall into Judah's lap. And very soon God will punish those who afflict Christians, revealing Jesus in consuming fire, condemning to eternal destruction those who refused to listen to the gospel of Paul. "In a little while" and "At last" come together here, appropriately because the texts derive from the Old and New Covenants. Still, the Pauline text stands alongside the prophetic one in awaiting the decisive act of judgment. But for both, God's timing was off, allowing foreigners to dominate the Jews in one instance and allowing Jewish hostility toward Christians in another instance.

For many of us, God's timing in the twentieth century seems completely askew. To salvage our faith in a benevolent Sovereign of the universe, we have taken the symbol of the Cross with utmost seriousness, concluding that suffering lies at the heart of God. Having abandoned the notion of power as the essential nature of Deity, we have claimed that God suffered in the kiln with dying Jews — indeed, that wherever calamity strikes innocent people, God is there, shedding the first hot tear. Perhaps that is why I recoil from Paul's eager anticipation of divine vengeance. Its timing is wrong, and possibly even more than its timing.

To be sure, the human desire to turn the tables on one's enemies makes sense, particularly when the foes lack moral and religious superiority. Haggai's contemporaries certainly had a score to settle with their rulers, who had stripped them of wealth and dignity. In 597 the Babylonian armies removed the valuable vessels from the temple at Jerusalem, and the later Persian largesse in no way replaced the gold and silver that once adorned the holy place. Now in dire economic straits, the few Jews who had returned from captivity to an unwalled holy city found life bleak and frustrating. "Where has the glory gone?" they must have asked. Then a prophet came to their rescue, not one who thundered like Amos and Isaiah, the lightning striking with every utterance, but someone who spoke apologetically and almost wholly in trappings of authority. I doubt that any other biblical text has so many oracular formulas. Three times we read "Thus has the Lord of Hosts spoken," and five times "Whisper of the Lord of Hosts." Besides these frequent signals that a prophet is at work, one encounters the actual designation of Haggai as prophet and an astonishing apologetic particle from God ("Say to Joshua and Zerubbabel, please!"). Such timidity on the part of God and prophet is unheard of elsewhere.

Haggai's words contrast mightily with their form, for a bolder promise can scarcely be imagined. First, he deals with the nostalgia that tends to cripple older people. "You are right," he says. "Things used to be better." This puny house won't begin to compare with Solomon's temple. The golden age recedes into the dim past; ours is an era of lesser metal or clay. Who cannot identify with that lament? "But be strong and work. Then God will fill this place with treasures hitherto unheard of, dwarfing even Solomon's temple." For anyone with a scrupulous conscience who would object to Yahweh's theft of silver and gold from the peoples outside Judah, Haggai counters that all earthly goods actually belong to the Lord. "Mine are the cattle on a thousand hills." Such a message naturally avails itself of ancient assurances: negatively, "Don't be afraid," and positively, "I am with you, my spirit standing among you." In a word, this house will be filled with *shalom* and *kabod,* peace and prosperity, splendor and glory. With these ancient concepts Haggai comes very close to proclaiming that the Lord will dwell in this place, as Ezekiel had shouted joyously, "The Lord will be there!"

The New Testament text also combines logical argument with emotional intensity fueled by apocalyptic imagery and implicit loyalty to a revered teacher who introduced the audience to the gospel. Here alone in the Bible do we find the word rendered "proof," a term rarely used in classical Greek: *endeigma.* Strange evidence, we may add, that nestles within hope, which is itself a matter of faith. In a word, Paul claims that the fulfillment of our thirst for vengeance against those who have abused us will suffice as decisive proof of God's justice. The terrifying appearance of Jesus will signal unending punishment for the unfortunate while ushering Paul's loyal friends into eternal bliss. One almost senses here the ecstasy described without apology in Second Esdras, where the saved lean over the clouds and enjoy seeing the discomfiture of the damned. We search in vain for the aching heart that prompted Ezra to protest lest the divine honor be sullied, or Moses in a similar situation to urge God to erase the name of the faithful servant from the book of life. Vengeance may belong to the Lord, but that doesn't make its execution any more palatable. When urged to make peace with his maker, Voltaire's dying quip captured more truth than he dared admit: "God will forgive — that's his business." But eternal damnation — is that God's proper business also? How do we reconcile this promise of revenge with God's readiness to forgive — yes, even to suffer death rather than resort to cruel force?

Not easily, I submit. Indeed, the texts for today stand convicted by a higher morality, one to which Abraham of old appealed in the stinging question "Shall not the Judge of all the earth act in a right and just manner?" Still, I join hands with the authors of the texts in pleading guilty before a higher tribunal. Why so? I have been ready to question divine justice — and sometimes even God's very existence — because of the delay in establishing justice on earth. The divine timing has not accorded with my assessment of things. Now the Pauline promise of eternal judgment that secures justice strikes me as unworthy conduct of the God whom I serve. It seems that when God wants to play ball, we have love on our minds; the result constitutes one cosmic joke, badly timed. Searching for justice, we observe divine long-suffering, and we wonder if neglect or indifference doesn't describe the situation more adequately. Pondering the prospect of divine vengeance, we object in the name of compassion. One might say, "You don't take sin seriously enough." Oh, yes I do, for that's why I take suffering to be the fundamental characteristic of God's self-manifestation.

Now if both the text and the reader stand condemned by a higher principle, we are obliged to search for explanations. Why do religious people invariably expect signs of divine favor despite overwhelming evidence to the contrary? Regrettably, most Christians come dangerously close to Tammy Fay Bakker's crass declaration that the tithe guarantees a pay raise, an income-tax refund, and a better job. Nearer the truth is the lone voice crying in the night: "Whom God loves, God chastens." From one perspective, I understand what prompts Haggai's triumphant vision of newfound wealth and Paul's certainty that God will zap the enemy, but my own experience leads me to value much more the psalmist's acknowledgment that such thinking mistakes God's goodies for divine goodness (Ps. 73). I shall therefore take my stand with this sublime thinker who determined to walk in the dark, confident that the Lord's hand led the way and that the only thing in the world worthy of desire was the abiding presence of God. On that reality and that alone can we rely.

We Must Give an Account
for All Our Deeds

Exodus 20:1-20; Romans 14:5-12

The very thought of accountability sends chills down our spine. Unpleasant memories rush through our mind — punishment as a child, whether a slapped hand or a look of displeasure on our parents' faces, or being deprived in one way or another of some desired good; discovery of deception or dereliction of duty as an adult, and the ensuing reckoning when we had to assume responsibility for our actions. Accountability is societal as well as personal. As a nation we face a reckoning for wasted resources, use of substances that destroy the environment, policies that bring death and suffering to other countries in the name of democracy. The hole in the ozone layer, acid rain, toxic waste crises, and impending holocaust daily remind us that we shall give an account of our deeds some day. In the words of a famous evangelist of another generation, "Payday someday!" Unlike those in high places today, we do not have the luxury of passing the buck to someone with less power and social standing. For most people, the thought of a reckoning remains totally alien. But it is a law of nature and of God. A day of accountability is coming. Even the most liberated book in the Bible, Ecclesiastes, concludes with a secondary tag-on affirming a day of reckoning when all hidden things will come to light. We cannot escape command, for law is essential to life.

One response to authoritative command is to soften its rigor by imaginative treatment. The rabbis spun webs of fantasy about the occasion at Sinai when divine law was first introduced to Israel's ancestors. According to one scenario, God first offered the law to the surrounding peoples, but they were unwilling to give up their belief in many gods, their fondness for images, their dallying with adultery, and so forth. In another version, God held Mt. Sinai over Israel's head and threatened the people if it refused to accept the Decalogue. The actual biblical account offers a nice perspective. God rescued a slave people and then gave them the Ten Words, which they received in gratitude. But other laws followed, and the rabbis tried to render them bearable. They imagined that the statutes numbered 613, of which 365 were prohibitions and 248 positive commands. From this fanciful numbering scheme, they fashioned a beautiful moral teaching that each day of the year brings new temptation to be resisted by a firm "Do Not!" and that the 248 members of the body lie in readiness to serve the Holy One.

Perhaps such imaginative treatment of the Decalogue was the rabbis' acknowledgment of the difficulties attending the text. The literary form mixes statements positive and negative, short and long, with motive clauses and without them. The context is ambiguous, running from the sublime to the ridiculous, from awesome theophany to such trivia as warning against touching a woman prior to encountering God, or exposing one's nakedness to the One who created the human body and declared everything good. The audience is unclear, and the language defies understanding in some cases. What is meant by no god besides me (in opposition to me?), sacred images (even as an aid to worship?), honoring parents (parents of adults?), abusing God's name (in magical rites?), killing (murder?), adultery (fornication?), stealing (a person's property?)? Why are only three warrants given, and why these three?

Leaving aside the complexity of the actual Ten Words, we do what later Israelites did. We soften the impact of divine command, which we sometimes experience as harsh. But not always, for discerning minds recognize the necessity of limits in our lives, guidelines that tell us what we can do with impunity and what we cannot do.

Listen to the marvelous attenuation of the Law's demands that is credited to Rabbi Simlai of the third century. Moses gave us 613 laws, and David reduced them to eleven (Ps. 15:2-5: "Whoever walks blame-lessly, does what is right, speaks truth from the heart, does not slander, does no evil to a friend nor reproaches one, despises a reprobate, honors God-fearers, swears to one's own hurt but is constant, does not accept interest on loans, and takes no bribe — that person will dwell on God's mountain"). Isaiah reduced them to six (33:15: "Whoever walks righteously and speaks uprightly, despises the gain of oppressions, shakes off bribes, refuses to listen to violence, and refuses to look on evil will dwell on the heights"). Then Micah reduced them to three (6:8: "God has shown you what is good, and what does the Lord require of you but to do justice, to love kindness, and to walk humbly with your God?"). Isaiah came again and reduced the number to two (56:1: "Keep justice, and do righteousness"; Simlai overlooks the following verse, which enjoins the keeping of the Sabbath). Then Amos reduced the number to one (5:6: *dirshuni wiḥyu'*, "Seek me and live"), and Habak-kuk confirmed this enumeration (2:4: "The just shall live by faithful-ness"). One is tempted to add that Joseph Askari of Safed (16th cent.) moved one step closer to the truth when asserting that joy is a necessary condition without which a law cannot be perfectly carried out.

Not everyone softened the requirements of the law. Despite an amazing laxity with respect to many specifics, Jesus is remembered in some circles as having insisted that the disciples' goodness exceeded that of scribes and Pharisees, whose observance of the Law, externally considered, was remarkable. Whatever Matthew meant by fulfilling the Law, whether bringing it to completion or perfectly observing its essence, he certainly gave divine command its elevated place.

For those of us today who take up Amos's challenge of searching for the Lord in order that we may discover life, Mt. Sinai stands between us and our destination. We see the dark smoke and hear the loud thunder; our knees buckle, and we see ourselves exposed before the light of day. Reckoning has come, and we wonder how many prisoners we have visited, how many naked we have clothed, and how many hungry persons we have fed. Dare we count on divine concession to weakness, as an unknown rabbi did?

God says to Israel, "I commanded you to read your prayers to me in the synagogues, but if you cannot, pray in your house; and if you are unable to do this, pray when you are in your field; if this is inconvenient to you, pray on your bed; and if you cannot do even this, think of me in your heart."

This is little, and it is much!

The Word Is Out

Exodus 2:11-22

I want to begin with a confession. I have spent much of the last three weeks trying to decide whether or not to preach on the lectionary text for today. Frankly, the story about Moses' murdering an Egyptian is troublesome, and his kindness in coming to the defense of damsels in distress hardly redeems the text enough to justify using it for spiritual guidance.

When I told a colleague about my dilemma, he noted that the problem was peculiar to Protestants, who emphasize the proclamation of the Word as the sacral moment of worship. "As an Episcopalian," he said, "I don't worry much about the sermon, for we believe that one encounters the Holy in the act of the sacrament." His observation lowered my anxiety level when I realized that today's sermon will be followed by a service of communion.

Of course, I could concentrate on the gospel lesson, although it offers ambiguous consolation. On the one hand, the parable of the sower (or, more correctly, the seed) calls attention to the considerable expenditure of energy and expense in proportion to the yield. What minister can take comfort from the fact that all sorts of obstacles hinder a successful proclamation of the good news? And what profit will you receive from my reminding you about those things in your lives and mine that prevent a wholehearted and joyous response to the gospel? Perhaps both you and I can console ourselves with the knowledge that the success of the proclamation is not, after all, left to human beings. Our words, however feeble and inadequate, will yield extraordinary harvest, thanks to the mystery of God's unseen presence. That is why I dare to stand in this pulpit today.

But to ignore the Old Testament lesson would be, for me at least, a betrayal of the part of the Bible that has nurtured my life for more than a quarter of a century. Therefore, I am determined to wrest something worthwhile from this unpromising account of Moses' disaffection with Pharaoh's court. I ask you to bear with me as I search the nooks and crannies of this familiar episode, a story that is more at home in Hollywood than in church.

Let us begin by paying attention to a few distinctions of language, for the vocabulary of the three episodes focuses the reader's attention on the tension between ethnic groups, Hebrews and Egyptians. Moses promptly strikes a lethal blow against an Egyptian, but when he sees Hebrews fighting one another he tries to reason with them. Ironically, the Midianite women to whose rescue he comes draw the natural conclusion that Moses is an Egyptian, presumably on the basis of his outward appearance. Underlying this tension between Hebrews and Egyptians is the assumption that Midianites were related to the early Hebrews. It seems that something more than religious differences governs the author's feelings; that something is nationalism. Moses reaches a stage in life when he must choose which side of the family he will opt for: the luxurious palace of his adoptive parents or the bondage of the mother who gave birth to him. Later, in Midian, he narrows that choice once more, for here he decides to defend the rights of an oppressed group of cousins. Presumably, the shepherds who regularly denied the young women access to the watering hole were Midianite cousins too, but the text does not actually specify who they were.

Several words stand out in this story. The first word is "murder." The Hebrew who informs Moses that someone had watched him try to conceal his violent act on the previous day uses the strongest term possible, after having asked who commissioned Moses to the grand role of deliverer: "Do you intend to murder us as you murdered the Egyptian?" The question about commissioning points forward to God's appearance in the burning bush. Moreover, the comment that Pharaoh tried to kill his grandson uses the same Hebrew verb for "murder," where one would expect something much milder (say "arrest," "imprison," or maybe just "talk with"). One gets the impression that this observation paves the way for an even more perplexing comment later in the book of Exodus: that at a lodging place on the way, God tried to kill Moses. I do not profess to understand this puzzling verse, but I am certain that the author wishes to set up a vivid contrast between two gods, Israel's God and Pharaoh, who was seen as the embodiment of evil in the story. Third, the allusion to shepherds as villains requires comment. The metaphor of the shepherd, widely used in the ancient world for God and the gods of various people, has etched itself into our memory through Psalm 23 and Jesus' parable of the good shepherd. Thus we find it hard to think of shepherds as villains in a story, but that's their role here.

One thing is crystal clear. The author describes a world out of joint, one peopled by corrupt rulers, oppressive taskmasters, quarreling slaves, murderous do-gooders, abusive shepherds, second-rate citizens (women, that is), and opportunistic parents. You and I may consider the specifics of the story strange, but we recognize the ingredients that constitute this broken world. We can barely restrain ourselves from turning the page in search of more comforting words, for we recall that the author observes in passing that Pharaoh died and that God saw the misery of the enslaved Hebrews and heard their cry.

Another thing strikes me as self-evident. The text defends the cause of individuals who suffer as a result of cruel or indifferent government officials. It urges us to identify with the weak, which hardly makes sense from any rational perspective. After all, those in positions of power and privilege are capable of making our lives comfortable and reasonably secure, but what can the disadvantaged do to help us? This way of stating the matter illustrates the problem, and that problem is our inherently selfish nature. Moses chose to ease the burden of slaves and to defend the rights of women. In that decision, he forfeited a life of ease and inaugurated a period of hiding in a wilderness far away. Something within him resisted human bondage, and this rage cost him dearly.

To be sure, it has become fashionable today to champion the

rights of ethnic minorities and women — at least in word. The deed is somewhat more complex. Moving from rhetoric to action requires infinite patience and immense powers of discrimination. Perhaps we shall make progress by listening to our text while at the same time recognizing its limitations. Joel's marvelous vision of a day when the divine spirit becomes universally present in strong and weak, male and female, children and the aged, is much more inclusive and therefore more acceptable to modern readers. The last two, children and the elderly, pose the greatest challenge for society today, and our text remains silent about them. I am aware that we cannot fully identify with all of these groups, but we can, at a minimum, lend our voice and vote to the powerless.

One further point pervades the text, although never coming to explicit expression. God also favors those persons who lack the resources for resisting cruelty. This lesson is a difficult one for reasonably affluent Christians to swallow, but liberation theologians have been pressing it for several decades. The Bible gave voice to a powerful strain of liberationist thought, for the prophets caught a glimpse of a reality beyond the usual scale of human values. In their view, God championed the cause of the poor and dispossessed victims of society. Naturally, these spokespersons for God came into conflict with persons who subscribed to the more popular thesis that God protected a godly state and its officials. We, too, struggle with competing views on this issue. We must be careful not to romanticize and idealize poverty, but at the same time we must not institutionalize a second-class citizenry.

How, then, do we act in such a jaundiced world? We must not be blind to the masks people wear, else we can be of no help. Like Moses' futile attempt to conceal his criminal act, masks fail to hide reality.

As much as anything else, our text deals with detection. In Jesus' familiar parable of the final judgment, the sick, the naked, the hungry, and the imprisoned represent Jesus on earth, so that a charitable deed directed to one of them amounts to a loving act toward Jesus. In this parable, the way we respond to need determines whether or not the gates of paradise swing open for us at death.

Nothing is said here about doctrine, the single issue that threatens to make a mockery of the denomination that nourished us. Jesus envisioned a moment when the masks fall off and our lives play on the heavenly screen. Others have reflected on that dreaded day of exposure in other ways. The prophet Amos spoke about an unspecified devastation that virtually wiped out the people, and a lone survivor urged silence lest God hear and complete the job. In a powerful version of this biblical anecdote, Elie Wiesel tells a story about a Jewish madman in a Nazi concentration camp who says, "Sh . . . we must not pray, for God will learn that we are still alive!" Exposure means many things, but it seldom points to something good.

Sadly, our society has gotten used to such unpleasant revelations; our heroes have clay feet. The champion of civil rights and the president who stirred youthful idealism were womanizers, Pete Rose had a weakness for gambling, and so on. When this happens again and again, we become cynical. Our president asks us to read his lips, only to convey an ambiguous message, prompting a cartoonist to depict a lipless president on his knees looking for them. In our society only the wealthy can afford to run for public office, and then they spend most of their time satisfying their affluent backers. Hence they seldom look after the well-being of the poor. We thus easily understand the story about a customer who took some cloth to a tailor and ordered a suit of clothes. When told it would take two weeks, the customer complained that God had created the world in six days. The tailor replied, "Yes, and look what a sorry job he did." Perhaps the blame is wrongly put, for *we* have certainly made a mess of things. For this reason, Christians refuse to surrender the vision of a better world, and until it dawns, we choose to walk the lonely path that Moses and Jesus cleared. At times we feel like the Jewish peasant who became lost in the woods at prayertime and despaired because he had no prayerbook. Nevertheless, he recited the Hebrew alphabet and trusted God to arrange the letters into a prayer as best God could.

Elie Wiesel tells about a Jewish survivor of the death camps who steadfastly refused to pray until he began to think about how lonely God must be now that Hitler had silenced the voice of those whom God loved. We pray for another reason too, and we stand alongside the victims of society, because, as a midrash on Exodus says, God appeared to Moses in a thornbush as an indication that suffering belongs to the divine nature itself. That insight places us squarely before the Cross, and we have at long last arrived at what Paul described as the heart of the gospel: the preaching of Christ crucified.

A Memorial Worthy of Jesus' Name

Joshua 3:7-17; 1 Thessalonians 2:9-13

Two recent events in the life of our nation have emphasized the widespread feeling that momentous occasions need to be remembered in an appropriate manner. I refer, of course, to the dedication of the memorial wall that honors those who died in Vietnam and the opening of the museum dedicated to the victims of the Holocaust. Visitors to these profound expressions of collective grief have experienced quickened heartbeat in breasts thought incapable of feeling ever again and have surrendered to the marvelous healing power of forgiveness.

Not every celebrative occasion designed to bring people together has such regenerative results. Witness, for example, inaugural parades down Pennsylvania Avenue marking transitions in office. For one thing, the defeated party licks its wounds, imagines what might have been if not for strategic blunders during the election campaign, and begins to plan for the next general election, when incumbents will surely be toppled. For another, backers of those being sworn in to official positions find themselves divided in victory, for spoils of office, however numerous and lucrative, are not sufficient to go around, and disgruntled workers gripe about being passed over by those whom they championed in adverse circumstances. What is more, both the lucky persons assuming office and their supporters sense the awesome task facing them and privately wonder if they can meet the challenge effectively when so many previous functionaries have failed. When one adds to all this disquietude the nagging suspicion among marginalized victims in society that such pretensions to royalty do not accord well with democracy, particularly the lavish expenditure of funds that could be targeted to alleviate human misery, the celebrations and prayer breakfasts ring hollow.

Similar ambiguity accompanied the change in leadership occasioned by the death of Moses. Even his loyal supporters conceded that not everyone looked on those early years in the bleak wilderness with fondness, despite popular belief in providential care. According to this recollection, Moses had always come through when his back was against a wall — or, more accurately, when his God had parted the waters of the Reed Sea to let escaping slaves walk to freedom and had brought mighty waters crashing down on Pharaoh's pursuing army. When a tired people, overcome by hunger and thirst, complained bitterly, his God supplied water from a rocky cliff and provided quail and manna sufficient to meet all their needs. Still, Moses' leadership evoked dissent from those closest to him, his own brother and sister, and his elevation above the crowd created too great a chasm between him and ordinary sojourners in hostile territory.

Will things be any different under Joshua's leadership? This question lies behind the account of the crossing of the Jordan River on dry ground. The larger context emphasizes the passage through uncharted waters, a powerful symbol for all transitions in leadership where an unknown and untried individual takes over the helm of the ship of state. The context also establishes a spatial buffer zone for the holy, in this instance the sacred ark, lest harm befall the careless or the curious who venture too near the symbolic representation of divine presence during its move from place to place. Perhaps the most important contextual signal, however, is the heightening of expectation residing in the promise that the much-heralded age of miracles has not come to an end. Thus the stage is set for yet another wonder, now as confirmation of new spiritual leadership.

Contemporary moviegoers, like ancient Israelites, have been captivated by the ark of the covenant and have attributed an aura to it that has generated considerable excitement. Audiences thrilled to the adventures portrayed in *Raiders of the Lost Ark*, which combined myths of evil and inordinate superstition. Both of these derive from biblical record and later Ethiopic legend involving the Queen of Sheba. The first story describes the death of Uzzah, who slipped while transporting the ark, accidentally touching it and suffering the consequences, whereas the second legend reports that Solomon's son by the Queen of Sheba persuaded Jerusalem's religious guardians of the ark to abandon that city in favor of the land of Sheba and to take the valuable ark with them. This tradition explains why the movie has its hero discover the ark in Egyptian sands, although in all likelihood it perished in flames when Jerusalem was sacked by Babylonian soldiers in the sixth century.

Above all else, this text about a change in leadership stresses continuity. That link with the past is achieved by replicating the singular miracle in the people's memory, the astonishing rescue from Egyptian soldiers. This new miracle is different in one sense: it is not occasioned by hot pursuit. Nevertheless, the crossing of the Jordan River on dry ground hardly takes place in a vacuum, for the wondrous act is interpreted as decisive proof that God will exterminate the inhabitants of the land into which Joshua will lead his people. The difference is temporal and spatial: the danger threatening Moses pressed in on him from behind, while Joshua's foes await his marching toward a permanent place of residence.

We note that the text offers assurance that the present miracle is a pledge of future wonders involving success in battle. The narrator refuses to let history retain its customary ambiguity, for the text promises certainty of victory. The wall of water, à la Cecil B. DeMille, removes the necessity for faith, inasmuch as only a fool would question God's promise after witnessing this miracle. A single remark gives the reader pause, however, suggesting that things were hardly so simple. That comment concerns the information that the Jordan regularly overflows its banks in the season of wheat harvest. To be sure, this observation calls attention to the awesome miracle, one that tames a rushing stream, but the comment also reveals the audience as people unfamiliar with the river in question. The story therefore arose in Babylonian exile, which reinforces our suspicion that its purpose is less historical veracity than religious indoctrination. Awaiting those who return to Jerusalem are hostile peoples who will resist anyone intent on reclaiming the land. Hence the vital concern: Will God help us expel these foreigners and recover our land?

The exilic period seems obsessed with acquiring conclusive proof, if the formula that Ezekiel used so often accurately reflects things in his day. The same concern permeates the rhetoric of the lyrical poet responsible for the comforting words in Isaiah 40–55, as well as the rhetoric of prophets like Joel, who proclaim a divine sign that removes all doubt that God has become present to the residents of the holy city. Knowledge is not all of one kind, however, and few could rest easy on the basis of such assertions. Hearing a description of a revelatory event, seeing the event, and experiencing it are quite different in themselves. The one who is caught up in divine fire knows its reality differently from the person who has only heard about it or even from the one who has merely seen the flame without being engulfed in it.

Once alerted to the apologetic nature of this story about the transition from Moses' leadership to Joshua's, we can discern other features that function in this way. Both the description of Israel's God as the "living God" and the twice-mentioned "Lord of the whole earth" address an exiled people perplexed by the apparent weakness of their deity or the alternative interpretation that the Lord has completely abandoned them. Even the mythic structuring of space points beyond a particular serpentine river to divine beginnings and catastrophic happenings. This must surely be the deeper meaning of waters forming a dam at Adam while God's people cross on dry ground at Jericho, far above the Salt Sea, to which the failed river wends its way and dries up.

We who struggle with uncomfortable biblical texts can certainly appreciate such profound sentiments, for the rarity of divine miracles led to frequent rehearsals of what God had done in former times. Nevertheless, the central promise enunciated by wondrous deed has left a dubious legacy that persists to this day. Indigenous peoples are driven from their homelands in the name of the Lord of the whole earth: Canaanites, Hittites, Hivites, Perizzites, Girgashites, Amorites, and Jebusites. For these unfortunate victims of religious enthusiasm no one erected a memorial like the twelve stones testifying to divine sovereignty. The companion New Testament text in the lectionary offers no comfort, for it also lashes out in a tirade against Jews in the same breath that it makes a claim to be divine revelation as opposed to human words. What a telling reminder that it takes more than mere assertion to validate a statement as the true word of God!

We have not gathered in this place today for the purpose of noting the faults of ancient worshippers, for that is relatively easy to do. Instead, we are here to confess our own sins, which are often illuminated by examining earlier responses to daily challenges. Above all else the lectionary readings convict religious people of gross insensitivity even during their exhilarating moments. We can safely assert that something is fundamentally wrong when assurance of divine presence issues in mass homicide and ethnic cleansing. Such ideology as that underlying the eradication of whole populations and the intemperate verbal abuse of brothers and sisters who disagree with us over religious issues places us in need of God's forgiveness. As I see things, assurance of forgiveness alone demonstrates the promise that God will be in our midst. Having experienced that gift of love, we can then take steps to make amends for all our misdeeds. That is surely the real meaning of God's presence — and the only memorial worthy of Jesus' name.

God and the Unexpected

Joel 2:1-2, 12-17a

As a child I was intrigued with the game of denominational one-upmanship and the comforting world it represented. In my denomination the biggest claim to superiority was security of the believers, known popularly as "once saved, always saved." To be sure, Christians sometimes backslid, but annual revivals were scheduled to persuade these lapsing believers to return to the path of righteousness. The flames of hell were very real in our imaginations, but this tidy system of security kept them in check. For us there was no element of surprise. We knew everything there was to know about God, and Christians were secure in the divine arms, but woe unto the sinner!

How far removed from this fantasy world is the God revealed to us in the Bible! Granted, the ancient Israelites tried to create a tidy world also, one where surprises found no place. For example, the story of the Flood concludes with a promise that God has placed the rainbow in the sky as a reminder that the forces of chaos must never again threaten civilization. On the face of it, this sign meant that nature would permit life to flourish, and the God who controlled nature's forces would guarantee it. The author of the medieval poem about the warrior's bow with the arrow pointed heavenward perceived this implication fully.

In due time the people of God coined a liturgical confession, placing it on divine lips and identifying the creed as God's special favor to Moses in lieu of seeing the Deity:

The Lord, Yahweh, a God compassionate and gracious, patient, and full of loyalty and integrity, keeping covenant love for thousands, forgiving offense, rebellion, and sin, *but* who will by no means pardon the guilty, visiting the iniquity of parents on the children and grandchildren, to the third and fourth generation.

This rehearsal of the thirteen divine attributes must have functioned widely in ancient Israel, for it crops up in various forms time and again. It is still a significant part of the Passover service today, when parents ask children a series of thirteen questions that conclude with reciting the biblical text from Exodus 34:6-7. "One, who knows it?" "One, I know it. One is the Lord of heaven and earth." "Two, who knows it?" "Two, I know it. Two are the tablets. . . ."

According to this confession, God was trustworthy. People knew exactly where they stood. God was both compassionate and avenging. Although the confession does not actually say so, it was taken to imply that good people experienced the favorable attributes and sinners experienced the unfavorable ones. Still, questions inserted themselves into daily lives, and believers pondered deeply God's nature. Three texts indicate the profundity of these examinations: Abraham's question to a God bent on destroying Sodom and Gomorrah ("Shall not the Judge of all the earth do right?"); the prologue of the story of Job (God endorses murder for the sake of a wager); and Jonah's prayer ("I knew you were a gracious God and compassionate, patient, and abounding in loyal love, and repent concerning evil").

The trouble was that God always introduced the unexpected, things beyond human calculation: preferring the offerings of a shepherd to a farmer's gift, selecting one family and its descendants, ignoring the right of the firstborn and choosing the youngest, hardening hearts that were eager to repent, sending armies against the chosen people, repenting of plans to punish a wicked nation that had brought untold misery against Israel. The tidy world of human fabrication kept receding. God refused to be enslaved, and humans often got the short end of the stick.

The text in Joel introduces us to yet another divine surprise, an action that is described as unique. A locust plague has devoured the food supply, but an even more dreadful spectre looms on the horizon. God has raised up an apocalyptic army that is poised to attack the people of God's choosing. We watch as desperate measures are taken: the sounding of the alarm, the blowing of the ram's horn that announced an approaching army, the running here and there, the checking of the ramparts, the mustering of old men and children, even the summoning of the bride from her chamber and the groom from his room, the frantic activity of priests. Then comes the prophet Joel, who appeals to the tidy world to ward off the untidy. "Rend your hearts and not just your garments. . . . Perhaps — who knows — God may repent, for God is gracious and compassionate, patient, abounding in faithful love, and repents of evil."

Here is the familiar liturgical chant, but used selectively. Missing are the threatening words, and in their place is a new promise that God repents of evil. Two things strike me as worthy of note: Joel concedes that God actually intends evil, and the prophet admits that authentic repentance may not reconstitute the tidy world we cherish. Three times this "who knows?" occurs in the Hebrew Bible along with the positive words of the ancient liturgy. When a sinful David explained his actions during the illness of the child of lust, he said, "I thought, who knows? God might have mercy and repent so that the child will live." But the prayer for mercy, cleansing, and renewed joy did not bring the desired results, and the child died. In the second instance, the Ninevites used the words "who knows" in wondering whether God would turn and repent so that they might live, and this time God did so, to Jonah's dismay. In Joel's case, we do not know whether God responded favorably to the torn hearts or not. Judging from the other two cases, the odds were even.

It seems that God was always determined to shatter every illusion of security. Then along came the lowly Galilean. Like Joel and others before him, Jesus insisted that God saw beyond external show where acts of benevolence and piety were concerned. "If there is to be dissimulation, let it be the kind that conceals one's true spirit of fasting, which God alone will perceive." "Your real treasure will be known to God, for your heart will be there." "Cultivate prayer in the secret places of your life. Then God will reward you." Commendable teachings, these.

And look what his reward was! Golgotha exploded every illusion of the tidy world, the security of the believer. The surprise was too much for the Galilean: "My God, my God, why hast thou forsaken me?" Whether it was a cry of dereliction or a confession from the Psalms, the words echo through the corridors of our soul, alerting us to the unexpected. This is the eternal *shophar*, the alarm that sounds throughout the city, bringing terror to our hearts.

Here is the real world in which we live. Earthquakes bury innocent persons in their rubble; famines leave millions with hollow eyes and bloated bellies; religious wars divide nations and squander young boys in fruitless conflicts; ruthless entrepreneurs traffic in drugs and ruin countless lives; disease and age take their ever-increasing toll; and power wields its stick even in the halls of justice. No wonder a perceptive rabbi once said to God on Yom Kippur, the Day of Atonement, "God, if you forgive us, we will forgive you too!"

But hold on. Before we point an accusing finger at God, let us acknowledge our own guilt. It is there. Perhaps I should speak for myself alone, for that's all I can speak about from firsthand experience. As one who is subject to sin's power, I tremble before the Lord of the Universe, for I can make no claim to special favor. In my life there are no guarantees, and I acknowledge that. My tears would be unbearable if they concealed another divine surprise: a tiny band of followers who willingly carry on the work that the Galilean began. Women and men, boys and girls, together are bringing healing to a tortured world. People are being changed, for an invisible power is at work in the lives of these ambassadors for Christ. The powers that rule this world threaten to extinguish the flame, but it flickers and jumps from soul to soul. Even my tears cannot extinguish the flame, and for that I am eternally thankful. It may be that God's supreme surprise is the privilege of drying someone else's tears and placing a comforting arm around trembling shoulders, for even repentant sinners who have no guarantee can do that much.

Emerging from the
Hot Furnace of Shame

Joel 2:23-30

Return with me for a moment to the playground of your youth. A voice rings out, strong and shrill because it belongs to a small band of taunters: "Na-na-na-na-na! Little Suzie Four Eyes!" From another side of the playground sounds a comparable song, this one uttered by boys: "Sissy-Sissy; Billy's a sissy. Sissy! Sissy! Sissy!" Now go with me into the shelter of home and listen to yet another kind of rebuke issuing from a parent's lips, from a mouth that has often kissed away the hurts endured on the playground: "Tommy, I'm ashamed of you for the way you acted today." Accompany me on one last journey, this one into the place of private prayer where the sense of shame is entirely self-generated, a pained awareness that we have experienced a moment of weakness that resulted in a word or deed causing pain to others. Who among us has not been thrown at one time or another, like Shadrach, Meshach, and Abednego, into the furnace of shame? Having shed hot tears of shame, we can appreciate the powerful feelings embedded in our text from the prophetic book of Joel.

No thanks, however, to the person or persons who chose the lectionary reading, which interrupts a divine oracle of assurance and then breaks off in the middle of things. It thus ignores the central paradox of the text and distorts the promise itself. Beginning the reading at verse 23 and concluding with verse 30 is like entering a theater in the middle of a play and trying to understand the dialogue and plot without benefit of key ideas and delineation of characters. Without knowing that the Judeans had become the object of mockery by foreigners, how can we sense the pathos underlying the twice-stated "And my people will never again be put to shame"? By what means will they be delivered from mockery? Through God's taking up residence in their midst. One can scarcely imagine a more daring thought.

For those of you who entered the theater in the middle of the play — and I suspect that includes almost everyone when the plot concerns the prophet Joel — perhaps a brief description of the program will be useful. The play consists of two acts. In Act I God calls everyone to lamentation — old men and women whose memory includes nothing comparable to the calamity that has struck the Judean countryside, young people who thought they had the world by the tail, and priests. God threatens them all with an invading army far more invincible than the locust hordes that decimated the land and left hunger in their wake. Whereupon Joel urges genuine repentance and holds out a remote possibility, though phrased as no more than a "who knows," that God will have compassion on those who rend their hearts. The basis for hope rests in God's essential nature, a forbearing, merciful, gracious, forgiving, kind disposition announced to Moses in a special moment. This first act ends with an assembly of people, even newlyweds and infants still nourished by their mothers' milk, and with priests addressing God in prayer: "Have mercy on your people, O God, and do not hand over your inheritance to be a byword among the nations, the butt of jokes. Why should they say among the peoples, 'Where is their God?'" With this great convocation the curtain falls on Act I.

At the beginning of Act II, the curtain rises to a resounding shout, a declaration that God took pity on the victims of mockery. Then come the transformative promises: the sending of plenty to vanquish want, and eradication of the sources of disaster, both actions falling into the category of miracle. Now God encourages the distressed land, sobbing animals, and joyless people. To each of these the divine exhortation brings consolation. "Fear not, O land, for God has worked wonders." "Fear not, animals, for the scorched pastures are being transformed with lush growth." The word to Judeans differs only slightly: "Be glad and rejoice!" The text for today begins here; it leaves off at the moment of terrible threat, this time spoken for the benefit of Jerusalem's inhabitants, who can now rejoice over their enemies' downfall. Stopping where it does, this reading omits the wonderful statement that balances divine calling with human calling, grace and works. Those who invoke God's name in Zion will be saved, together with some survivors whom God calls, as promised. The final "as promised" holds together divine and human initiative, affirming all the while the reliability of God in the face of overwhelming evidence to the contrary. Daily starving in the Judean hills persuaded neighboring peoples that God could not be trusted — indeed, was powerless to do anything about it. Act II unfolds the mystery of concealed divine power as nations make a pilgrimage to the valley of decision and submit to God's judgment. The act closes with a crescendo: "Revenge is sweet indeed."

The dramatic plot involves the remarkable transition from being an object of mockery to being confident that the God who was ridiculed as powerless or disinterested in Judah's fate actually resides in its midst. That is not all. This God is the only one there is. What a bold and daring claim in the face of reality. You and I live in a pluralistic society comparable to ancient Judah's religious smorgasbord. Our daring claim that God exists strikes many people as the height of folly, a throwback to earlier superstition. In most intellectual circles, theism stinks, and its adherents are subjected to the modern equivalent of the foreigners' taunt directed against Jerusalem's citizens. Their assertion that the Lord was the only true God was astonishing in a world that boasted a host of gods. Conscious of the precariousness of such a confession, the scriptwriter attributes the audacious denial of other gods to Judah's own deity, who declares that all doubt will be overcome: "And you will know that I am in Israel's midst; I am Yahweh your God, and there is no other. You will never again be put to shame."

As expected in plays of this sort, villains get what they deserve and heroes emerge victorious. This reversal is accomplished through amazing deeds. We aren't told how the destruction of locusts, God's mighty army, actually takes place, only that God has acted wondrously. Appropriately, the people sing praises to their deliverer. The play ought to end here, but it does not. What follows introduces some unstable elements into the action. God promises to break some long-standing barriers: agism, sexism, social class, religious privilege. An ancient promise to Moses will finally be realized, and access to God's vitality will become universal *in Judah*. Previous distinctions will crumble like the Berlin Wall. Boys and girls will prophesy, old people will discover the divine intention in dreams, young adults will have visions. Slaves will experience this divine disposition just as free people do. The only fly in the ointment is the restriction of God's spirit to Judeans, but that small limitation should not minimize the extraordinary achievement. Four out of five constitutes a very acceptable batting average.

The flaw in the dramatic plot is the prediction itself, not its narrow base. The sole function of prophecy was to provide mediation between Transcendence and mortals — that is, to convey God's will to human beings and to communicate their cause to God. What need of either exists when God dwells among the people? Obviously, this brief textual unit disturbs the flow of action. Whence did it derive? Perhaps it arose in the dark ponderings about God's dwelling in pure light but enveloped in darkness. Here we have the attempt to encompass both the mystery and the revelation of God, the eternal mystery that conceals at the same time it divulges essential being. Those Judeans who might become comfortable with the notion of "God with us" are forced to contemplate awesome portents in the sky and on earth; the image of "mushrooming smoke" has become an apt one even for moderns who cannot erase the picture of Hiroshima and Nagasaki from their minds.

Yet another Judean community of faith appropriated Joel's remarkable promise of an outpouring of God's spirit, this time without national boundaries. At the same time, this new group acknowledged the mystery accompanying "God with us." There is neither Jew nor Greek, male nor female, bond nor free — all are one in Christ. Marching words, these, but society marches to a different tune, one that emphasizes those features that separate us. Where will it all end? In the name of removing shame, we have ironically strengthened its grip on us. We are caught in an inescapable net fashioned by two contradictory impulses: exclusive allegiance to the only God, and a universalizing inclusion of all God's creatures. The one breeds intolerance; the other, pluralism. Until this situation changes, tears of shame will flow down our cheeks, Joel's comforting promise notwithstanding. It is precisely here that my greatest quarrel with the extent of the lectionary reading occurs, for it omits the image that concludes the original word from God. The grammar and syntax stress continuous action; God calls us by name. We are being called to salvation, being summoned to build a fellowship on earth that unites mystery and revelation, presence and absence, in such a way as to embrace saint and sinner, Judean and foreigner, and all such polarities that alienate God's creatures. We will not escape the furnace of shame until every "na-na-na-na-na" vanishes from our midst and in its place everyone affirms the wonderful deed that surpasses anything we could ever imagine, "God with us." When that miracle happens, we can return once more to our childhood days, but the children will be singing a different tune: "Jesus calls us. . . ." Amen and amen!

And There Was No More Sea

Revelation 21:1-5

The text for this morning possesses rare power to stimulate the imagination and stir the heart. Its unparalleled vision lifts us above the humdrum existence of ordinary affairs. Born in the agony of human suffering, the injustice perpetrated by a power-mad Roman emperor, the torture of mangled bodies and spilt blood, this prophetic vision perceives a hidden reality above and beyond the chaos of the present. Refusing to allow unprecedented persecution to weave a veil of resignation over his spirit that would cripple him with debilitating skepticism, the author rises to noble thoughts and creative insights. But not without paying a price — the vision was slow in coming, and was preceded by an orgy of bitter hatred scarcely justified by attributing it to divine wrath. We shall forego discussion of the baser reaction to suffering, limiting ourselves to the sublime expression of final salvation.

Seldom does the unity of the Bible find expression so richly as in the vision of a new heaven and a new earth. Jew and Christian join one another both in recognition of their limits and in faith that God alone can bring redemption. The vision is couched in Old Testament language and imagery, while presupposing familiarity with Israel's narratives of creation in Genesis 1 and 2. On the basis of linguistic usage, we can surmise that the prophetic vision found in Isaiah 40–55 spoke to the author with singular force. Small wonder, for this poetic masterpiece also sprang from the humiliation and frustration of Babylonian captivity. Jerusalem's collapse and Israel's demise prompted serious soul-searching, and prolonged misery elicited hope in a new Jerusalem — indeed, a new creation where former saving deeds could be forgotten since overshadowed by novel acts of God, who comes to dwell in Zion.

Let it be noted that the text constitutes a vision. The author knows the power inherent within a vision about final salvation. Israel's proverbialists warned that without a vision the people perish. Each of us draws daily upon a precious vision, dreaming the impossible dream, striving for the unreachable star, surrendering to our unique quest. The tiny gap between the actual and the ideal keeps us humble and contributes the challenge essential to active living. For the poet, that vision amounts to a perfect phrase; for the occasional athlete, a round of par golf. The physician dreams of a correct diagnosis of a rare disease; the parent envisions a son or daughter equipped for coping with reality. Visions vary in quality just as sharply as they do in content. Faust's final lofty thoughts — about the taming of the restless sea for society's benefit — approach the grandeur of the biblical text. Here we read about a new beginning, an unspeakable presence, and a majestic victory.

I. A New Beginning

"Then I saw a new heaven and a new earth; for the first heaven and the first earth had passed away, and the sea was no more. And I saw the holy city, New Jerusalem, coming down out of heaven from God, prepared as a bride adorned for her husband."

While the first creation had been pronounced exceptionally good by its Maker, still something was amiss. Sea, serpent, and seduction constituted a fatal flaw. Hence anticipation of a new creative act arose early.

All of us know something about the grip of the new upon our lives. We express a fascination for novelty in various ways: we celebrate New Year's Day with resolutions we know will be broken before the day is out, and we submit to baptism as a symbol of the cleansing of sins, although we know most of them will crop up now and again. All our relationships eventually become tarnished, and we long for a clean slate. Sometimes the baggage of memories is too much to contend with, and, sloughing off the old, we enter into new marriages, new friendships, different jobs, strange locations. Often we become addicted to the new, habitually laying ourselves open to false starts in the hope that we shall eventually discover the perfect spouse, the ideal job, just the right place. Then we risk becoming jaded, so that our fascination with and surrender to the new loses some of its appeal. Still, the text speaks with unforgettable power — it proclaims the arrival of the truly new, a universe that is pristine, pure, perfect.

Small wonder that marital imagery pervades the text at this point. The holy city, New Jerusalem, descends from above clothed in a bridal veil, pure as new-fallen snow. The old city, despite her splendor, had never lived up to expectations. Ever present was the disparity between the ideal and the real, the sacred and the profane. Holy men and women, God-like boys and girls, walked her streets by day, and the basest criminals stalked them by night. The gulf between what she was and what she ought to be grew progressively greater or smaller, waxed and waned. That guardian of things holy, Jeremiah, combed the city of Jerusalem looking for one righteous person, and like Diogenes with his lantern, he searched in vain. Still, Israel's traditions spoke of Jerusalem as God's special city, the symbol of divine presence, and recalled miraculous deliverances at the eleventh hour. Now at last Zion becomes a holy city, and the unknown author of Isaiah 40–55 is vindicated, for her name becomes "The Lord is there."

II. An Unspeakable Presence

"And I heard a loud voice from the throne saying, 'Behold, the dwelling of God is with mortals. He will dwell with them, and they shall be his people, and God himself will be with them; he will wipe away every tear from their eyes. . . .'"

We have now moved from vision to audition. A royal herald proclaims the unutterable: God's dwelling is with men and women, boys and girls. So overcome by the wonderful news is the herald that he has difficulty containing himself, repeating the key phrase that God will dwell with them, God in person. Behind this proclamation rests an active tradition, one with constant tension between a God closer than the smallest whisper and farther away than the farthest star. This mystery of divine presence prompted boast and lament: boast that the Lord dwelt in the holy ark, lament that God visited the tent of meeting only when choosing to do so. At stake was divine freedom, a freedom from human manipulation for man and woman's own needs. Perceptive souls made the issue exceptionally clear, and even the Solomonic temple was conceived under such tension between divine presence and absence. God dwelt in heaven, but the divine name resided on earth. The author of Stephen's last speech in Acts had drunk deeply from the cup holding these traditions; God, he insists, has always been on the move. Jesus, too, only tabernacled in our midst according to a significant New Testament tradition.

Here, again, the author casts a furtive glance at the early Genesis story. There God is said to have walked regularly with human creatures in the cool of the evening. Even these leisurely conversations terminated when sin intruded. Hereafter rare souls walked with God or talked with the Creator face to face. All others cringed before the Lord in dread, begging the Judge to depart hastily. Now all that terror is past, and fellowship is restored at last. Hence Hosea's indictment of Israel is nullified, and once again God calls her a chosen people. A single, remarkable consequence of divine presence suffices, for it speaks volumes. God passes the time drying tears! This simple dramatic gesture, the gentle touch of a parent, says as much about God as the story of Jesus' washing his disciples' feet does. Fundamentally, it declares once and for all that the sea is no more.

III. A Majestic Victory

The herald continues: "And death shall be no more, neither shall there be mourning nor crying nor pain any more, for the former things have passed away."

This marvelous assurance returns to the theme we have chosen to emphasize in the text: and the sea was no more. In Jewish symbolism the sea was the embodiment of evil, the source of chaos and destruction. From it came bestial rulers in Daniel's vision, and in it the primeval Chaos Monster lurked and cavorted, ever threatening to swallow the forces contributing to order, reason, and sanity. The sea's tentacles touch us all at one decisive point — death.

Originally death, in Israel's view, was an act of gracious compassion. It was God's means of preventing estranged creatures from living forever; that is how we must understand the old story about God's driving sinful humans from the garden in which stood the tree of life. We certainly are not to view this story as God's zeal to keep the best things for divine use alone. Once trust in God's sustaining arms collapses, death becomes an unbearable yoke. Sirach's half-humorous epitaph ("Mine today, yours tomorrow") hardly conceals the sting of ultimate extinction when we come into our inheritance of maggots and worms.

For some of us, as for Paul, death manifests itself daily. We cry when others suffer physical or psychological hurt, we mourn when others die of starvation, we hurt when estrangement and alienation separate God's creatures, we wail when ignorance crushes truth. We experience both the agony and the ecstasy of divine suffering and love, and we long to be free of such travail. Like Albert Schweitzer, we moan that only at quite rare moments have we felt really glad to be alive, for we know Robert Penn Warren was right in observing, "Oh, it's real. It's the only real thing — pain. So let's name the truth like men. We are born to hope that hope may become pain. We are born to joy that joy may become pain. We are born to love that love may become pain. We are born to pain that pain may become more pain." In truth, the history of humankind can be summed up in three words: born, suffered, died.

The vision relegates all this to the domain of former things — for the sea is no more! Death's bitter sting is removed, as are its manifestations. Vanished are pain, tears, sorrow. They disappeared along with the tears God wiped away from swollen eyes. Now at last nothing obstructs our vision of God, and nothing else matters in all of creation.

Appropriately, the text leaves its earthly setting behind and concludes with God's promise that the vision will not lie, the words will not deceive. "And he who sat upon the throne said, 'Behold, I make all things new.' Also he said, 'Write this, for these words are trustworthy and true.'"

These final words have a sobering effect, preventing us from escaping into grandiose visions. Recalling as they do the terrible story of the test God administered to Abraham, they raise the fundamental question of human existence: that of divine integrity. The divine promise that God can be trusted falls with jarring impact. It reminds us of the distinction between human and divine words, even in so grand a vision, and forces us to ask who really speaks in the text. Is the vision of a new beginning, an unspeakable presence, and a majestic victory God's comforting word or human misguided escape? I wish I could assure you that these words, at least, were conceived in God's heart and fell from divine lips. But, alas, I cannot, for I would then be untrue to the text itself. The tone of the final promise betrays the fact that the author wrestles with doubt, his own and another's. Although wishing to suppress it as quickly as possible, the author permits just a hint of skepticism to remain in the final vision.

Doubt, like adversity, can both destroy life's nerve centers and prompt soul searching that keeps us honest and creative. In good measure, skepticism tempers our hope that someday, somehow, truth will prevail, sorrow will be no more, and God will be all in all. That tiny element of doubt compels us to live as though the vision depended upon our own efforts at transforming the universe. At the same time, we draw constant nourishment from the belief that a new day will dawn, and the sea will be no more. It will have dried up along with the tears of God's children, whose elbows are too weak to push others around and whose hearts ache on account of universal human misery.

Father, we are beggars, that's for sure.
Filled, we hunger still — not for food and drink —
but for Thee alone.

Grant us vision; give us hope.
Dry our tears so we can see others' moist eyes,
perchance thine too!

Then until our dying gasp we shall render thanks
to the One who makes all things new, without the
boisterous sea!
Amen.

A Divine Love Song

Isaiah 5:1-7

All the world loves a lover. Or so we have been told. Perhaps we secretly admire anyone free enough to throw caution to the wind and to act on something so fragile as a feeling, so uncontrollable as passion, so uncertain as fondness for another person. Love's fragility frightens most of us, for we observe its shattered pieces in our own lives and in those of people around us. Its control of our actions for both good and ill makes us hesitant to surrender fully, for we prefer to maintain control over the course of our lives. Love's unpredictability engenders fear in us lest our tender expressions of endearment encounter resistance or even rebuff. In spite of these hindrances to love's abandon, many of us charge ahead, considering the advantages of loving and being loved greater than all the undesirable possibilities. Experience teaches us that love thrives on hope — indeed, that it seldom exists apart from anticipated bliss. The realities of the moment, often harsh, become bearable because we know that something even greater awaits lovers. In time, and after much effort, two souls become one, a reality that persists even though two distinct bodies and wills also continue to seek expression. Knowing this, we smile when we observe love blossoming, whether in our own lives or in those of acquaintances.

Seldom, however, do we extend that exhilaration over love's emergence among human beings to include the Source of all life, the One we worship as Creator and Redeemer. Our reluctance to do so springs from the biblical tradition and its cultural context. Religious people throughout the ancient world celebrated divine love between male and female gods, and in their own liturgical response they tended to seek a means through which they could lay hold on the extraordinary power associated with such love. For some reason, biblical interpreters of divine and human relationships resisted this popular expression of linkage between the transcendent realm and the human one. Their God, they insisted, had no consort, no lover with whom to bring the world into being, but existed as an entity unto itself. One unfortunate result of this emphasis was its negative impact on women, one that only recently has elicited strong resentment and, in some circles, a return to the ancient form of worship featuring god and goddess. The Catholic Church, of course, early tapped into this old source when Mary was elevated to a status just short of deity. Protestantism, however, refused to endorse this way of dealing with human longing for female representation in heaven, however much it shared the desire.

Astonishingly, rare poets and bold prophets in ancient Israel imagined God as lover, although such thoughts opened the floodgates through which popular concepts of divine male and female lovers rushed unchecked. Moreover, such notions invariably came embedded within images of nature's lush growth, which evoked lavish rites under shade trees and provoked bitter prophetic denunciation. In the judgment of the prophets Hosea and Ezekiel, such worship invited sexual license — indeed, abandon. Each worshipper sacrificed virtue from a deep sense of religious devotion. In New Testament times the same practice continued at Corinth, with similar motives, and stirred up Paul's anger. When the unprecedented venture into such dangerous territory first occurred, the poets and prophets dared to link God emotionally with the people of Israel and Judah. God was envisioned as husband of one or two wives, neither of whom honored the marital relationship. Never for one moment did the prophets understand this metaphor literally; instead, the language of husband and wife functioned as an effective way to express intimacy, to convey the strength of the covenant bond uniting people with God.

The lure of the erotic attaches itself to the beautiful song of the vineyard attributed to the prophet Isaiah. Its form — alternating voices — gives a false impression of cool detachment, which its content quickly belies. The prophet adopts the role of a minstrel and begins to sing about ill-fated love, but the divine lover suddenly takes up the tune and gives free expression to an ardor that has transformed itself into hot anger. After the love song has faded into an awful threat, the divine lover adopts the sure sign of love's disappearance: silence that signals an end to all communication. At this point the prophet takes up the song once more, identifying lover and beloved so that no one in his audience could miss its terrifying message.

The image of God as gardener is almost as bold as that of God as lover. After all, according to the creation narrative in Genesis 2 and 3, God placed the man and the woman in the garden and assigned its care to them. The symbol of a garden runs through the Bible. The garden of Eden tells the story of paradise lost, witnessing both to the possibility of love for another but also to its distortion into self-love. The garden that serves as a bed for lover and beloved in Song of Songs attests to paradise regained on the human level, although one listens in vain for any acknowledgment that human love finds ultimate fulfillment when focused on life's source. The garden of Gethsemane proclaims divine love as the source of our redemption, its scope extending to the final vision of a new heaven and a new earth in Revelation. The centrality of the image of a garden has achieved expression in the single river that flows from the holy temple and in the tree of life growing alongside that stream. The divine gardener finds joy in the simple chores of planting and harvesting. Small wonder that children discover such pleasure in observing the miracle of growth from once dormant seeds.

When grapes grow in the garden, joy abounds, for wine was known to enrich life appreciably. In Israel wine was actually a mainstay of daily diet as well as an offering to God. Given these facts, biblical writers saw nothing improper about describing God as a vintner. The prophet painstakingly describes God's wooing of the people. God chooses the most fertile land available, digs holes large enough to accommodate the growth of a healthy root system, cleans away all rocks that would deter growth, plants select vines, builds a tower from which to watch for invasive animals, carves out a wine vat in the tower, and sits down to wait for a bountiful harvest. No vintner could be more attentive to a vineyard; no lover could woo a beloved more passionately. Such a faithful lover had every reason to expect rich reward for expended effort. Sadly, proffered love, however passionate, does not automatically create a response in kind.

God's threat is grounded in the disparity between faithful wooing and contemptuous response. "You be the judge," God urges the people, "between me and you. What more could I have done?" Twice God contrasts the expected favorable response with what really resulted: useless grapes that stunk. The offended lover has no mercy, threatening utter destruction. God will demolish hedge and wall, stop pruning and hoeing the vines, allowing briars and thorns to take over, and withhold rain.

Having shifted from first-person prophetic address to first person divine address, the prophet returns to talking about God. The Lord of Hosts — here the martial imagery is intentional — has a vineyard, the people of Israel and Judah. When God looked for justice, criminality came into view; when God searched for right dealing, the cry of oppressed victims like the murdered Abel rose from the earth. Here is a rare instance of poetic craft: a play on words. Looking for *mishpat*, God encountered *mispah*; expecting *sedaqah*, God found *se'aqah*. Another noteworthy poetic feature is the threefold use of the verb for "expecting," a patient waiting that now is past. If love really is always bittersweet, in this instance the bitter leaves a strong taste that puts to shame contemporary country music hits. This biblical love song ends on a vindictive note. That response to unreciprocated love is bad enough when it comes from human beings. Such harsh retaliation on God's part is deeply troubling.

An ancient Israelite also saw something unseemly in Isaiah's description of God and composed an alternative song of the vineyard, one that eventually found its way into the prophetic book of Isaiah. This new song, Isaiah 27:1-6, also reaches back into ancient religious concepts and personifies evil in the same way Babylonians and Canaanites had done. This use of mythic creatures to symbolize the embodiment of chaos that must be defeated by the Creator who then imposes order is but one of many such occurrences in the Bible, especially in texts about creation within Genesis, Psalms, Job, and Isaiah 40–55. From one perspective this symbolism amounts to human refusal to admit fault, like the fisherman from Mesopotamia who had no luck and concluded that his wife must have committed adultery. In his mind, one could reason from punishment (in his case, no fish) to offense (he knew he was not guilty). In such a worldview it was convenient to posit evil outside the human arena. That solution to unreciprocated love shifts responsibility from God's people and opens the door for further acts of love on God's part.

The earlier martial imagery returns here: the Lord seems to ask for a fight. First, the ancient mythological foes must be vanquished. Hence God readies a powerful sword with which to slay the twisting serpent Leviathan and the primordial monster residing in the sea, Tannin. Whether the poet envisions one or two creatures is unclear, given the parallel structure of Hebrew poetry and the slippery names attached to the creature(s). This poet stops short of later speculation about the saints feasting on Leviathan at a banquet marking the inauguration of God's kingdom.

Once evil has been vanquished, the Lord proceeds to sing again of a pleasant vineyard, now returning to first-person speech. The lusty singer brags about abundant signs of love: God waters the vineyard regularly and guards it, watching over the vines by night and day. It seems that this passionate lover gets bored easily, resenting the idyllic tranquility. Sensing a need to feel anger toward someone or something, this God wishes for briars and thorns. In other words, God wants to demonstrate ardor by overcoming resistance, burning these enemies of the grapevines. Then it occurs to God that destruction is not necessarily the only response to resistance — indeed, not even the best approach. The alternative is reconciliation, and the Lord proclaims an invitation: "Let them make peace with me." Lest God's enemies miss the words because of terror before one so powerful, God repeats the invitation, urging them to take hold of God as one clings to a place of refuge.

The prophetic voice returns at this point, promising a flourishing vineyard that will fill the whole world. The poet's exuberance leaves little to the imagination: roots will spread out, vines will send forth shoots, blossoms will appear, and finally fruit will ripen. Here, too, the poet takes pains to identify the vineyard with God's beloved people. In this scenario, the fruit is exactly what the keeper of the vineyard awaits. Only gardeners fully appreciate the excitement accompanying this reference to a successful harvest.

When we pause long enough to reflect on the way both songs describe the lovers, the reason for the presence of such different treatments of love becomes clear. They depict the twin realities of conditional and unconditional grace. The first song pictures God as an aggrieved lover; the second portrays God as an aggressive lover who will permit nothing to frustrate divine love. This tension between justice and mercy pervades the biblical witness. God demands an obedient response to the divine will made known in the Mosaic law and in the teachings of prophets and sages. What happens, however, if in their willfulness, humans spurn God's directives and return disrespect for faithful love? Left unchecked, this waywardness will actually defeat the divine intention for creation. God also pledges to bestow favor even on human beings who choose to go their own way. This means that God will accomplish the divine purpose regardless of human response, for such love as that expressed in divine freedom is mightier than its human counterpart.

The two songs also reflect the tension between present reality and future hope. We all try to balance these two: the harsh experiences of brokenness that inevitably characterize existence in space and time, and the wished-for perfection awaiting us beyond temporal and spatial limitations. Our fleeting moments of shared ecstasy point beyond the present frayed encounters to a union in some unknown future, a oneness resulting from mutual passion. In a word, we love God because God approaches us in loving reciprocity. The two songs explore both sides of this human dilemma, our present bondage to sin and our hoped-for deliverance from self-centeredness.

Happily, neither song glides over unpleasant circumstances. Love, however precious, remains highly ambiguous. In the story of the garden of Eden, the lovers must reckon with the sinister figure of the serpent, and in the narrative underlying Song of Songs, the two lovers must deal with a powerful monarch whose lust threatens their bliss. Calvary's shadow looms over Gethsemane in the same way. Human freedom is essential if love is to remain uncoerced, but divine compassion alone enables love when so much exists to hinder its free expression.

Confronted with the prospect of such love that overlooks human frailty and overcomes even the fiercest resistance without lashing out in anger, we can hardly restrain ourselves from joining in the ancient song about a keeper of the vineyard who loves freely and unconditionally. At the same time, our knowledge that love implies faithfulness enables us, however faintly, to sing along with Isaiah. If we know our hearts, we really do want to love God. That part is easy; however, our way of showing that love is purely earthly. We have to do justice and to practice righteousness toward our fellow human beings. Failure to express our love in concrete actions on behalf of the marginalized victims of society is in itself convincing evidence that our love for God is bogus. Jesus came to the same conclusion and warned his followers that participation in the hope of eternal life was dependent on our treatment of men and women, boys and girls. Dare we count on the reliability of that second song even though Jesus opted for the first and said nothing about the second one? An even bolder thought: Does divine compassion extend far enough to encompass resistance of Leviathan itself? That is, will all who are evil ultimately become recipients of divine grace? If that is in fact the implication of the Cross, how can we refrain from shouting from the rooftops, and how can we ever silence the song in our hearts?

"Whispered Sweet Nothings"

Hosea 2:14-23 [16-25]

A recent episode of *Prime Time Live* dealt with the agonizing problem of Alzheimer's disease, presenting a rare look at its effects by an intelligent woman who chronicled the changes in her daily activities brought on by the loss of distant memory. She told of having to keep maps of familiar landmarks along nearby streets to help her take the simplest kind of trip from her house to visit a friend who lived only blocks away. Telephone numbers — indeed, numbers of all kinds — had become a major difficulty for this woman, who once had held mastery over the most complex figures imaginable. Naturally, the drastic changes in her life put a strain on her marriage. In a particularly poignant moment, her husband, who was having an understandably difficult time coping with a woman quite different from the one he had known for years, was asked if he planned to stand by her and look after her as the disease progressed. After a noticeable delay, he said that he did, prompting his wife to ask, "Why didn't you tell me that?"

Traditional wedding vows include a promise to love the spouse for better or for worse, in sickness and in health, until death dissolves the relationship and releases one from the solemn oath. Illness is not the only thing that tests the resolve of those who have committed themselves to one another for life. The prophet Hosea takes us into the bedroom and exposes a wife's infidelity, wanton conduct that threatened to destroy a relationship that had witnessed the birth of three children. The complexity of the injured husband's feelings matches that of interpreting the prophet's message to idolatrous

Israel. Pain and anger unite, leaving a mighty scream in the night all too familiar to spouses who have been forced to reckon with an unfaithful companion. To forgive or not to forgive: that is the question. Making peace in such circumstances is not easy, as illustrated by the recent agreement between Israel and the Palestine Liberation Organization. Prime Minister Rabin's eloquent remarks accentuated the agony of signing a peace accord which came too late for those who lost their lives and which, to some, fails to remember their sacrifice in an appropriate manner. Reconciling husband and wife when one of them has been untrue to the bond uniting them resembles such peacemaking.

The decisive issue in the book of Hosea is even more complicated than settling marital disputes or martial conflicts. Here the bond between God and Israel has ruptured as a result of spiritual unfaithfulness, leaving God with a decision to make: whether or not to terminate the covenant relationship. As spokesman for the aggrieved partner, Hosea exposes an ache within the divine heart never before seen with such clarity. Anyone who has ever forgiven a faithless lover knows something about the painful self-examination attributed to God. "How can I give you up, O Israel?" The further reminder, "For I am God, and not a mortal, the Holy One in your midst" (Hosea 11:8-9), points to the complicating factor in the deliberation: the unknown effect of being unevenly yoked together. Holiness demands one thing, compassion yet another. How, therefore, can God reconcile the two attributes without being untrue to either?

The times in which the prophet Hosea lived were characterized by political chaos resulting from Assyria's resurgence to power in the area. During the three decades from 750 to 721 B.C., the prophet witnessed frequent changes in kingship and the inevitable collapse of Israel. Invasion by Assyrian soldiers led to widespread misery and excessive taxation. Foreign domination resulted in religious corruption, the customary surrender to alien cult practices honoring victorious gods. A defeated nation drew the logical conclusion that its God was weak and consequently not worthy of worship. For success in agriculture, the heart of the economy, the people called on gods other than their own. Difficult times thus threatened the bond uniting the people and God. When a beloved turns to others for affection, what can one do? After all, love cannot be commanded. It depends on mutuality and reciprocity.

Hosea adopts the boldest means possible to convey his message to the people. He marries a woman (perhaps two different women) of questionable morals, knowing that her conduct will make mockery of the bond uniting them. His knowledge of human nature is accurate, and Gomer quickly takes up with lovers, even bearing children to them. The prophet lets her proceed in this fashion long enough to provide an eloquent message that can scarcely be misunderstood. This wayward wife symbolizes Israel, and Hosea represents God. The names of their three children — "Jezreel," "Not pitied," and "Not my people" — communicate the divine word of judgment on a faithless nation. The message is unambiguous: Israel has betrayed the Lord and will pay for its adultery by being cast off and abandoned.

Unhappy with this ending to the story, someone — whether Hosea or a later editor is not certain — rewrote the story to create a different ending more compatible with a gracious God. In this version, God determines to win back a lost love. How does one do that? By wooing her as before. The text does not shrink from depicting God as an ardent lover whispering sweet nothings in the beloved's ear. Returning to the wilderness, the lovers will once again establish a relationship of mutuality. Now God can speak to Israel's heart, tenderly, without competition from other suitors. The language of wooing is highly charged, *pātāh* being the usual verb for seduction. The same verb is used to refer to enticement by Samson's wife and by God in Jeremiah's hard-hitting attack against a Stronger One who had, in his eyes, abused the relationship of messenger and sender. Furthermore, this text in Hosea seems to contradict the traditional account of Israel's experience in the wilderness, which was remembered as an unpleasant sojourn rather than a time of innocent honeymoon. Now that locale becomes a door of hope instead of a valley of trouble, and Israel will respond in the same way she did in her youth. Gone are the behavioral patterns acquired in adulthood. Hope, although unseen, is sure. Such a simple narrative, and yet what a miracle it describes!

Having announced the Lord's future activity, the text proceeds to highlight two important consequences of God's decision to regain a faithless love. First, she will undergo a radical change in speech. Her language of address will be altered so as to avoid the hurt communicated through frequent reminder of her previous affairs. Furthermore, even the terms of endearment between God and Israel will be changed. Gone forever will be the language of subservience, the Baal names. We must recall that in Israel husbands were addressed as "my master"; now wives will call their husbands "my man." Even nomenclature signals oneness and mutuality at last.

This new relationship will also witness a renewed pledge of affection, here indicated by a covenant with all creatures on earth and in the sky. The vulnerable bride will have nothing to fear, for the Lord promises to banish hostile predators from the land, breaking sword and bow. She can lie down to rest in security, knowing that the Lord watches over her. The new vocabulary extends to positive dimensions. God betroths her in righteousness, justice, compassion, lovingkindness, faithfulness, and knowledge. For Hosea this last term, "knowledge," functions as the most intimate of all, because it conveys sexual relations. Nevertheless, one looks in vain for the normal expression for love, 'ahabah. Having boldly pushed this language of marital intimacy to the breaking point, the author stops short at this decisive juncture.

A second radical change will take place as well. A new chain of communication will be set up to prevent misunderstanding and to assure dialogue between the loving couple. At that time the Lord promises to be available at all times and thus to respond when requests are made. This seeking and answering extends throughout the whole universe, including heaven and earth. The interrelationship between the skies and the ground, broken as a result of unfaithfulness, will be restored, and periodic rains will enable seeds to germinate in the warm soil and will allow plants to reach maturity without stress brought on by lack of moisture. The three essential products of agriculture — grain, wine, and oil — will once more bring joy to one and all.

This rich promise leads to an even greater one. The Lord will take over the farmer's task, sowing seeds in the good earth and watching over the harvest to see that it comes to fruition. This act signifies a shift in God's manner of responding to an unfaithful spouse. The harsh invectives have entirely vanished, and in their place issue words of solace. The sowing of seed (the meaning of the name *Jezreel*) will no longer signify a destructive battle, and the negative will be removed from the names of the other two siblings. "Not pitied" will be called "Pitied," and "Not my people" will be named "My people." The final word consists of a virtual dialogue of love, with the Lord saying to Israel, "You are my people," and with Israel addressing the Lord with the simple and direct "My God."

When we stand back and reflect on this remarkable conflict within Scripture itself, we marvel at its honesty. The breach of trust reflected in adulterous acts is serious indeed, and the hurt lingers long after it has been patched up and the couple has returned to former status. One's initial reaction to infidelity arises from the outrage of betrayal and wounded pride. Thus lashing out at the guilty spouse in anger is the most easily understood reaction to infidelity. That is how Hosea first envisions God's response to Israel's idolatry. Holiness must not be trampled on with impunity, for that would set a dangerous precedent.

Deeper pondering of the dilemma revealed an even greater ambiguity, one that gets at the heart of the problem. Does love cease when it becomes inconvenient, and when unreciprocated? What kind of love chooses self-advantage as its criterion? According to an eloquent tradition reflected in the book of Deuteronomy, God's love for Israel was not based on merit and had nothing to do with whether or not the people deserved such compassion. Instead, the Lord chose an unworthy nation and heaped lavish affection on it. The logic of a relationship based on such outpouring of goodness should lead to quite a different response than irate vengeance. A union founded on divine largesse ought to engender grateful response on the part of the one who receives such favor, but in the event that the exercise of love fails to evoke proper gratitude, does the initiator of the relationship have the right to demand affection? That kind of reflection surely underlies the second account of God's response to a wayward spouse.

This time God's constancy despite human frailty shapes the reaction. Having freely given love, God chooses to bestow pardon as well, speaking tenderly to one who has betrayed loyal affection. The message proclaimed in this reading of the situation transcends all attempts to calculate merits and to keep a tally of wrongs. In this text one comes close to the Apostle Paul's powerful praise of love that suffers long and is kind. The text from Hosea does not suggest that this response to infidelity, spiritual or otherwise, is an easy one. To the contrary, the divine struggle over the proper response that the book of Hosea exposes in all its pathos suggests that we who hope to imitate God will have our resolve tested to the limit.

Let us return to the story of the husband whose wife was suffering from a debilitating disease. The pathos of the relationship is obvious to everyone. Hence we do not wish to judge the husband harshly for pondering its implications for him. Yet the failure to communicate his intention to his wife on his own helps to focus the difference between human and divine love. God's love manifested itself to us in that while we were sinners, Christ died for us. The divine agony described by Hosea is consistent with such self-giving love.

Dream On, Brothers and Sisters!

Isaiah 61:1-9; Luke 4:16-21

U nlike Freud, I don't know much about dreams. This much I
do know: in the Bible they evoke ambivalent responses. On
the one hand, they may come from God as special revelation, while
on the other hand, they may arise in the imagination of wicked
persons. My own dreams merge past and present, alpha and omega.
They recover long-forgotten places and times, and they link both
with present friends and locales. Almost without exception, they
occur in the little village of my childhood, as if this place were the
star from which compass readings must be taken. There my children
play, as I once did, and there many of you, my friends, make an
appearance. Upon awaking, I imagine that the newly created scenes
and friendships from then and now swiftly vanish, unfortunate victims of open eyes. Our text belongs to that dream world.

How so? First, it brings together at least four different pasts
and presents: Third Isaiah's and that of his audience; Jesus' and his
hearers'; Luke's and his readers'; and ours. We sense different messages
at each level, as strange images emerge and then escape into the
shadows: Third Isaiah proclaiming to imprisoned debtors a Jubilee
year, a time when all debts are canceled and the prison doors are
flung wide open; Jesus startling the people in a synagogue by announcing that *today* this particular text has come true; Luke interpreting Jesus' sense as a frontal assault on Jews, whom the Galilean
reminded that God sought out a Syro-Phoenician widow for special
care when countless Israelites were perishing from hunger and thirst
and that the Lord healed Naaman the Syrian of leprosy although

leper colonies languished in the promised land; and our willingness to believe that this ancient promise amounts to something more than a delusion, the ever-recurring famine in the land of promise that an obedient Abraham first experienced and the faithful prophet Amos predicted. How many generations' hopes and dreams parade before our very eyes in this text generated by Second Isaiah's powerful poetic proclamation of comfort for an exiled people! Why is it that religious language, like lovers' discourse, always exaggerates? Despite grandiose promises, returning peoples found little comfort in poverty. Jesus' townspeople scarcely noticed any change in things while he walked among them. Luke the evangelist felt the necessity to come to terms with a new national clientele for the gospel. And we still find at least a trace of poverty in society, a few broken hearts, and one or two persons whose eyes are blinded by greed and power. Readers past and present must hear one constant refrain: "Promises, promises, nothing but empty promises."

Second, the text resembles a dream in that the identity of the speaker seems to shift from moment to moment. Four images surface and dart away before assuming actual flesh and blood. The initial soliloquy echoes prophetic vocation, although the emphasis upon the spirit residing within points in yet another direction — that of charismatic judges like Samson, who granted deliverance by conquering the oppressor. To be sure, Micah did boast of spirit possession, but this present text misconceives the prophetic role. In Second Isaiah those who stood on the watchtowers, not prophets, were privileged to announce glad tidings. In truth, the reference to divine anointing points beyond judges to kings, for the proper object of anointing was the ruler, and in later times, the priest as well. Small wonder that the text hastens to describe the people as priests, who will be supported by the foreign population. At long last the promise in Exodus will be realized: the people have become a nation of priests holy unto God.

Third, the vagueness of the message is reminiscent of patches of dreams one manages to salvage when sleep merges into wakefulness. Symbols flit in and out of the imagination with abandon, like the sparrow that inspired the Hebrew word translated "liberty." Hopes are raised, then dashed summarily. Political aspirations that arouse bitter feelings toward oppressors are generated with guarded language. The poet seems to think the mere proclaiming of deliverance effects it, just as temple singers in Chronicles are said to have defeated mighty soldiers by chanting God's praise. Still, the striking message harbors good news for people whose lot was burdensome, even if the image of God pasting a Band-Aid on a broken heart sounds bizarre — strange, that is, to persons unfamiliar with the description in Psalms of God as the Exalted One who binds up the brokenhearted and who accepts the contrite spirit as a suitable sacrifice. The eyes of unbelievers will be opened wide so they can behold God's vindication. Unfolding before their gaze is the sign of God's favor lavished upon former prisoners: yearlong goodwill as opposed to a swift day of vindication upon the oppressors. Nothing short of a new era will suffice to describe this unfolding drama. Sheer delight prompts the poet to tickle the fancy with a marvelous example of paronomasia that cannot be reproduced in English *(pe'ērl'ēper),* to give those who mourn in Jerusalem garlands instead of ashes. At this point the imagery trails off into the natural world: the mantle of praise will replace a failing lamp, and God's beloved will be called oaks of righteousness, so strong and so full of life are they. Planted by the Lord, they will stand until time immemorial, and their cities will be rebuilt once again. Foreigners will make double restitution for theft and will do slave labor for God's people. Suddenly the divine word breaks into the scene, and God promises perpetual happiness. Those who mourn now can rely upon this promise, or so the text affirms.

What has happened here? Human promises fade away and in their place come divine assurances. Are we not still in a dream world where humans and gods intermingle, and where unpleasant dreams vanish upon waking? Is the Easter season vastly different? We come to the old familiar story once more, just as Third Isaiah returned to his story of redemption, and we juxtapose its proclamation of good news with stark reality around us, as he also did. Anxiously, we search beneath the barren surface for hidden messages, clinging to each discovery as to newfound treasure. Try as we may, we cannot escape the suspicion that those with weak elbows and broken hearts, like the poor, will always be trampled into the dust. In saner moments we know that visions of unbroken bliss are pipe dreams, that liberty ever flits away before our very eyes. Does not the gospel alert us to the fact that suffering has entered the very heart of God, and doesn't the Bible proclaim a God who accompanies us into the prisons and knows what it means to mourn for someone precious beyond description? In light of this profound mystery, those who persist in dreams of paradise regained would do well to stand momentarily before the scandalous claim: today this Scripture has come true. From that vantage point, what fools we are to believe that assertion. Yes, what fools!

When God's Silence
Is Better than Speech

Habakkuk 1:2-11

Some books have extraordinary capacity to lift the human spirit and to engage the mind. That is true of the little book of Habakkuk, when it is read with understanding. To help you do so, I want to share with you my thoughts about the book in the hope that you will come to appreciate this prophet's legacy as much as I do. To be sure, one cannot take a text that was written 2,500 years ago in an entirely different culture and set it down in the twentieth century without doing injustice to both human communities. And yet in some ways Habakkuk seems wholly modern. My aim this morning is to help all of you see something of the grandeur of the text that has captured my heart and kept me captive for the last several months.

History has been rather stingy where Habakkuk is concerned. We know nothing about the prophet other than what is credited to him in the three chapters. From them we know that he lived roughly during the time of Jeremiah, a crucial period in the life of the people who saw themselves as God's chosen nation. Even Habakkuk's name is uncertain, for the Greek text calls him Ambakoun. Perhaps this paucity of real information about him partially explains why later legend tells about an unusual meal that he cooked in Jerusalem and served hundreds of miles away in Babylon to a hungry Daniel who had been thrown into a lions' den.

The book of Habakkuk owes its present form to the needs

of the worshipping community. Not only does it include a couple of disturbing prayers and responses to them, but it also has five threats against evil ones and a majestic hymn. Twice within the threats we are required to purify our minds from even the hint of self-exaltation. Once we are assured that the earth shall be full of the knowledge of the glory of the Lord as the waters fill the sea, and later we hear that the Lord is in the holy temple, and in hushed expectation we are urged to let all the earth keep silence in such presence.

The use of this book in worship long ago suggests that ancient Israelites faced life's difficulties much more openly than the contemporary church is willing to do. We live in an age when easy answers are served on silver trays for hungry souls, a time when religious charlatans amass fortunes by appealing to the human desire for simple solutions to life's perplexing problems. While we spend our waking hours engaging in petty infighting over trivial matters like whether or not the Bible has any historical errors, the whole world suffers poverty, disease, and loneliness. Perhaps Habakkuk can expose this sorry spectacle masquerading as true religion and point us to the way we can see beyond our own petty struggles.

The prophet experienced a crisis in his religious conviction. He could not understand why foreigners freely suppressed the people of God. Having been taught that the nation was especially chosen, he saw no evidence that such was the case. Rather than surrendering his religious convictions, he took them to God in prayer. His was no ordinary prayer, but one filled with doubt and perplexity. Habakkuk begins with a universal cry: "How long?" What he really wants to know is whether or not God cares what happens to the chosen people. "How long will you stand idly by while cruel men spill blood?" Of course, this cry echoes through the corridors of human history: "My God, my God, why have you forsaken me?" From early Christians who were facing death for others' sport, to women accused of witchcraft, to Jews in Europe and blacks in the United States, the same cry has bounced off the heavens. This is the awful request for information: "Will it never end?" "Can we count on help at some time in the future?" If so, perhaps we can hold on just a few days longer. In a word, is there any hope left for us? In our own way, who among us has not uttered Habakkuk's heartrending prayer?

Astonishingly, the prophet answers his question in a manner that only increases his anxiety. Here is where God's silence is better than speech! Habakkuk becomes convinced that God is actually rousing a nation that will punish the Assyrians, who brought about the prophet's complaint in the first place. However, these Babylonians will be even crueler taskmasters. In this instance, the treatment is worse than the disease itself. Habakkuk imagines that these mighty Babylonians will be cruel beyond belief, and that they will be irresistible as well. If he thinks justice has become twisted under the present circumstances, it will become that much more so when the Babylonians arrive, for they establish their own brand of justice, and they worship their own might.

Small wonder that the prophet wanted to understand why God strengthens such cruel people. So we hear a second prayerful complaint from his trembling lips: "Why do you allow relatively good people to fall at the hands of those who are more wicked than they?" The prophet knows that his own people are far from perfect, but he also knows that some of them try to practice common decency. Why, then, must they die when their murderers are totally devoid of goodness? This, too, is the universal cry when innocents perish and worthless people thrive. Is there one among us who has not uttered this cry at some time or other? It is a protest against wasted lives, the early death of a loved one who might have brought so much happiness to others, now forced to endure great loss for no apparent reason. At its very heart this is a question about the way God runs the world. From our perspective, God is not doing a very good job.

It seems that Habakkuk is not sure how to answer this difficult question, for he gets mixed up about whether the answer is a vision or an oracle, something seen or heard. Furthermore, the text is awfully corrupt, so that we cannot be sure exactly what it means. One thing is clear: the prophet believes that survival depends on being faithful to God. The operative word is simple: righteous people will live by being faithful. In other words, he realizes that God's actions defy human understanding, but he also believes that this is no reason to give up in despair. Therefore he concludes that even this mysterious God deserves his trust in spite of everything.

We have not heard the last of Habakkuk's frustration. Convinced that evil people will eventually pay for their deeds, he endeavors to find comfort in thoughts about their downfall. The scenario consists of five acts:

1. plunderers will be despoiled;
2. houses built by force will cry out;
3. towns constructed by bloodshed will go up in smoke;
4. those who give others wine for lecherous purposes will drink the cup of God's wrath;
5. idols are dumb, lifeless, and cannot reveal anything.

Naturally, these threats function to reinforce Habakkuk's religious convictions, which have suffered as a result of current events. The final hymn also offers another reason for trusting God. It describes the God of sacred memory who fought at Israel's side. Although Habakkuk realizes that times have changed and such a God is no longer believable, he wishes to keep the memory alive. Thus he pictures the Lord doing battle with the Egyptians and the Canaanites, a memory so compelling that Habakkuk shakes with terror, and so realistic that he decides to wait in hope for God to live up to what others have said about the Ancient of Days. Again, who among us has not experienced the disparity between what we have been taught about God and what we actually experience as real? And yet we continually surrender to the power of sacred memory, reciting the story anew in the hope that the very telling of the story will make it come true.

In the beginning I said that the book of Habakkuk can lift the spirit and engage the mind. So far we have concentrated on the powerful appeal to the intellect. Now I want to talk about Habakkuk's capacity to inspire us to nobler conduct. The book closes with one of the most remarkable statements in the Bible:

Even if the fig tree fails to blossom,
   and no fruit appears on the vines,
the produce of the olive fails
   and fields yield no food,
small animals are cut off from the fold,
   and cattle are missing from the stalls,
yet I will exult in Yahweh,
   I will rejoice in the God of my salvation.

In a word, the prophet who has just had his religious convictions shattered by reality speaks the unspeakable, utters the great "nevertheless" of faith. I may have no food in the pantry and no prospects of any, yet I will still praise the Lord — nay, more than that, I will truly experience joy in the God who defies human understanding.

The older I get, the less certain I become about everything, particularly the profound mysteries of life. That is true even though others around me seem to harbor no doubt about the things we have been taught from childhood. I watch as human beings suffer and die, and I can see no evidence that good people enjoy God's special favor. Indeed, it often seems that persons with sensitive hearts and weak elbows bear their own form of the Cross of Calvary, and that stark reality forever fills my lips with the two questions Habakkuk laid in God's lap: "How long?" and "Why?"

The suffering that I see on every hand is only half the picture, however; for I also witness acts of love and caring that equally defy understanding. That is the secret to the amazing power of sacred memory, and that is why we who dare to ask God about the way the universe is run also lift our eyes in adoration and praise. In the final analysis, the prophet who came to question God tarried to worship. That is what I invite you to do today.

Will Anyone Serve God for Nothing?

Job 1:9; 2:4; 9:23; 24:12

In Book II of Plato's *The Republic,* Socrates' pupil Glaucon denies the possibility and goodness of pure justice. "All men who practice justice do so against their will," he contends, "of necessity, but not as a good." Glaucon goes on to say, "I want to hear justice praised in respect of itself. Such a man will be scourged, racked, bound — will have his eyes burned out; and, at last, after suffering every kind of evil, he will be impaled." The learned pupil's last word is that such justice does not contribute to human happiness, and therefore is not good.

Glaucon casts his vote in favor of a universe operating on the principle of strict retribution — that is, he has fallen prey to the magical assumption that lies at the heart of all religion as we know it. Based on a simple syllogism, it can be described as follows. Major premise: right conduct pleases God; minor premise: God rewards that which pleases Deity; conclusion: therefore, the good person fares well in this life. The negative of this syllogism is likewise accepted: evil behavior angers God, the Deity punishes those who offend divine honor, and the evil person fares ill in this life. The logic is irrefutable; but the working out of the dogma brings untold anguish, agony, and heartache.

The magical assumption pervades the stories of sacred history and colors the pages of contemporary biography. Father Abraham argued with God on the basis of the assumption "Shall not the Judge of the whole earth do right?" and youthful Jeremiah likewise used it to get the better of a God who had failed to adhere to the magical assumption. The anonymous authors of Deuteronomy and Chronicles wrote and rewrote the history of Israel on the basis of this assumption, oblivious to the inadequacy of such a rubric, unaware of the untold anguish brought about by the application of such a principle to sacred history. The closest disciples of Jesus accepted its validity ("Master, who sinned, this man or his parents, that he was born blind?") and employed it for personal gain ("Lo, we have forsaken all; what will we receive?"). And the church learned her lesson well — in her hymnody ("It Pays to Serve Jesus"), her tither's day speeches ("How I gave a tenth and quadrupled my income"), and her superpatriotism (God must prosper America, for we are a chosen nation, as our coinage and pledge of allegiance to the flag remind God). All this without a single glance at the arrogant confidence of Israel, God's chosen people ("With us is God — no evil can befall us"), and her tragic history, or a solitary look at the Cross, on which was hanged the Chosen of God ("My God, my God, why hast thou forsaken me?").

For those whose hearts are hardened, encrusted, enslaved by the magical assumption — and that includes nearly all of us — ultimate beatitude is "the purring of comfortable souls under the tender strokes of a divine hand," symbolically portrayed in the hope of heaven for the good and the satisfaction of knowing that the evil will get their desert in hell. If this is the essence of Christianity, then Feuerbach is right — religion is an opiate of the people, and we ought to get up this very instant, walk out of this place of worship, and never give another thought to God.

But could it be that Feuerbach is wrong, that there is more to religion than the magical assumption — indeed, that the magical assumption is faith's worst enemy? Perhaps an answer can be found in the lives of those who suffered most because of this assumption! Our text tells of a man who stands for Everyone, one strangely like you and me in that he could find no comfort in a future life, for his ancestors had not given it a place in their tradition, and we can no longer believe it.

The tragedy, the anguish, indeed the pathos of Job is that he accepts the magical assumption. His agony is intensified by the

presence of three friends, miserable comforters, representing tradi-
tionalism, conservatism, and dogmatism, and reminding him with
every verbal blast that he has sinned and is being punished. Calling
to his attention, moreover, their goodness over against Job's, for *they*
are *healthy.* As if the presence of these accusers is not sufficient
torment, the young Elihu appears, his mind uncluttered with information, ably qualifying him to speak authoritatively on world affairs,
religion, and science.

Job senses the absence of God in his life, but not as a vacuum.
Rather, he feels it as an unavoidable Presence, an inescapable
Punisher. His confidence in his own goodness leads him to deny the
validity of the magical assumption. The major premise that God is
pleased with goodness falls by the wayside as Job hurls the charge
against God that the Deity does not delight in goodness (7:20: "Even
if I sin, what can I do to You, O watcher of mortals?"). The minor
premise that God rewards the good deed goes down, too, when Job
contends that God does not reward the righteous (24:12: "From the
city the dying groan, and the soul of the wounded begs for help; yet
God pays no attention to [their] prayer"; 9:23: "When disaster brings
sudden death, [God] mocks at the calamity of the innocent"). The
conclusion that good people fare well in this life, too, no longer
stands (9:24: "The earth is given into the power of the wicked; [God]
covers the faces of its judges — if it is not he, who then is it?").

Job has become convinced that the times are disjointed, that
God is sitting in heaven mocking the victims of wanton cruelty,
hiding divine eyes from human suffering, encouraging the oppressors
by prospering them. Who among you at one time or other has not
been compelled to draw similar conclusions, has not felt the burden
of a dawning realization that human suffering cannot be explained,
has not sensed the incongruity between moral excellence and suffering? Indeed, who has not in his or her most private thoughts concluded that God is either powerless or unjust?

The grim reality forced upon Job by the magical assumption
is that God is unjust. In Job the colossal human ego bares itself: God
has hidden because of fear to face me at the bar of justice; indeed,
God will be sorry when it is too late. Job has concluded that the

world doesn't spin according to the magical assumption, so he wishes to get off. He even dares to make fun of Scripture, parodying the eighth psalm and the creation story ("What is man, that you spit on him?" and "Let there be light, my eye — let there rather be darkness"). The language is excusable; as a recent commentator has remarked, the sounds one gives out when celebrating dropping an anvil on his big toe have a ring of eternity.

The author of the book of Job does not despair, however, after dealing a death blow to the magical assumption. This was left for the writer of Ecclesiastes to do, to whom there was no congruity in life at all, no ultimate meaning in religion, work, wisdom, wealth, or sex. Rather, this genius discerns that Job's suffering is not punishment, but possesses the possibility of redemption. It was obvious that Jesus had read his Scriptures well when he said that the blind man was suffering through no guilt, but for the glory of God. Herein lies the secret perceived by the author of Job: suffering is an inexplicable mystery, but it may become a vehicle for the manifestation of the kingdom of God on earth.

Job has lost the god of magic and is confronted by the Lord of reconciling, forgiving, transforming love. This god who appears in the whirlwind may slap the rump of the hippopotamus, but God descends to converse with a hurting man about his agony, to deal seriously with his anguished cry. The distance between God and humanity is not removed, for God cannot be controlled by goodness. Nevertheless, the nearness of God is maintained, for the Lord comes in forgiving love, ready to transform him who had dared to blaspheme, to accept the doubter as a creature of integrity. Job confronts the God behind god, who does not offer carrots or sticks, who refuses to surrender divine freedom to any logical syllogism.

A comparison of two individuals at prayer may bring into sharp focus the conflict between magic and faith. Enter the closets, if you will, of two men in their hours of communion with God, the first from the beginnings of the people of God, the second from the inception of God's new people. The scheming Jacob, having stolen the blessing and gained by defraud the birthright, flees from his brother and pauses to ask divine sanction: "If you will go with me, protect me from my enemies, keep me healthy and make me wealthy, and at last bring me back home in peace, then I will give you a tenth of all my possessions, and you can be my God." Contrast, if you will, the lowly Nazarene's prayer in the Garden of Gethsemane: "Lord, I don't want to die; I much prefer to live, get married, and reach a ripe old age. Nevertheless, speak the word — I am at your disposal: not my will, but thine be done." Give me; take me! This is magic versus faith! And lest you draw the erroneous conclusion that I mean by this Old Testament versus New Testament, Judaism versus Christianity, note that the suffering servant of Isaiah 40–55 asks nothing and gives all, and that the three Hebrews in Daniel, facing death by fire, vow to trust God whether they are delivered or not. Now Satan's question has been answered: "Will anyone serve God for nothing?" Yes indeed: "Though he slay me, yet will I serve Him." And his creed can be rewritten: "All that a man has he will give for his life" can now read "All that a man has he will give for his God." Here at last is a stance from which the mystery of human suffering may be transcended. Now we can live with undeserved suffering, confident that God may come to us in reconciling love.

The Church Fathers record the story of a prophetess parading through the streets of a city, a torch in one hand and a pail of water in the other, her words ringing out over the murmur of the curious crowd enslaved by the magical assumption: "Would to God that I could put out the fires of hell with this water, and burn heaven with this flame, that men would love God for himself alone." Her summons has come alive this morning, and you are confronted with a living message, met with a demand to decide today, to make a response in magic or in faith, not because of fear of hell or desire for heaven, but because the living God has summoned you to life here and now.

The Cross: From Stumbling Block to Major Asset

Acts 2:14a, 22-32

Travel with me backwards in time to Jerusalem — to the fourth decade of what later came to be known as the Common Era. Together we confront a strange world: a language that sounds funny, weird clothes, a slow, uncomfortable mode of travel, crude houses, entirely alien customs. Strange though these things are, most likely the strangest of all is the sermon that Peter preaches in response to a linguistic phenomenon: the reversal of the experience of the Tower of Babel. His argument would be minimally acceptable at Vanderbilt Divinity School if we were in a generous mood. What faulty logic! What bizarre exegesis! What ad hominem reasoning! Besides, the sermon lacks those features that enrich an interpretive endeavor in our eyes: attention to structure, form, and context; examination of traditions and motifs; analysis of aesthetic and sociological features, deep structures, and so on. But we must not be too hard on a rude fisherman, for he lacks the training essential to the ministerial task. Should we, then, be grateful to him for giving us an example of what not to do?

First, the gaps in logic. Peter recognizes the stumbling block confronting the new movement, as yet unnamed. The leader has been rejected by his own people, publicly exposed, and executed by Roman soldiers. These unwelcome facts have collided with raised expectations, messianic in texture, and have elicited the pluperfect admission: "We had hoped that he would be the deliverer!" Combating such defeatism, Peter seizes the initiative, claiming that God has borne witness to Jesus' life. Never mind the silent heavens when mobs demanded his crucifixion! And the even silenter heavens when he implored *"Eli, eli, lama sabachthani"* ("My God, my God, why hast thou forsaken me?"). How did Peter think he could get away with such an egregious falsification of events that were common knowledge? His tactic: an appeal to special knowledge about God's intention. Beautiful! The Cross was no accident, no demonstration of God's disapproval, but precisely the opposite. (Reminds one of Paul's argument that reverses values, extolling foolishness and weakness as God's special way of achieving the divine goal.) In God's foreknowledge, everything was planned. "If you don't believe me," says Paul, "then listen to Scripture."

Then comes the bizarre exegesis. Peter shifts from a general observation (God planned things) to a specific instance. This is tricky business. Quoting Psalm 16, Peter notes that David prophesied those very events. Here the argument becomes ludicrous. Ignoring the actual thought expressed in the Hebrew ("I behold the Lord continually, who will not allow me to see corruption"), Peter latches on to the Septuagint translation because it confirms his beliefs. (Modern interpreters who insist on using the King James Version because its theology is pure can appeal to Peter's example.) Whereas the psalm actually observes that God will not permit the psalmist to succumb to Sheol's power, the Septuagint ignores the synonymous parallelism and inserts the idea of a holy one, which Peter understands to be Jesus. Nothing in the text suggests the leap from holy one to Jesus, but this does not deter Peter. Indeed, he asserts the impossible: that God raised Jesus from the dead, loosing the bonds restricting him to the underworld. To be sure, the utterances of devout persons paved the way for the astonishing claim: Job's heartrending cry, a hopeless wish that the grave could not hold him, and the poignant confession in Psalm 73 that the bond uniting creature and Creator will somehow endure through the ages, "for God, my everlasting rock, is all I want."

The ad hominem argument follows: we are witnesses to the resurrection. Suddenly we begin to see how Peter has employed Greek rhetoric and fashioned a ring composition, God's attestation and human witness joining a celestial chorus. Jesus lives! Perhaps we have judged Peter too harshly. Let's leave that to Paul. To be sure, the faulty logic, weird exegesis, and ad hominem argument remain. But what else? In a word, Peter examined Scripture in the light of his understanding of God and his experience, daring to fashion the sacred text on the basis of changing circumstances. When Scripture fails to correspond to reality, reinterpret Scripture. This principle underlies Peter's sermon, and it is entirely legitimate.

Of course, we would be happier if Peter had been faithful to the psalm, for it has two concepts that capture the human dilemma. The first acknowledges the fact that human existence takes place within certain constraints. The most we can do is hope for redemption, living in anticipation. Hence we shall dwell in hope. That is little, and it is much. The other image points to a hidden dimension which underlies that hope. We experience full joy in God's presence. As Faust perceived, the mystery of the resurrection is first and foremost a claim about believers, who experience God's forgiveness and hence are reborn. Such was not Peter's experience, although it is mine.

What does Peter's sermon teach us today? That we all do the same thing in trying to make sense of reality in light of sacred texts? Perhaps more importantly, that Christianity depends on hearts *and* heads, the evangelical witness *and* the doubting thought. We can stay at one another's throat and preside over the demise of Christianity, or we can begin to accommodate the special concerns of both extremes. That task, I believe, is the supreme challenge facing us in the twentieth century. Reading Peter's sermon dramatizes the immensity of the chasm separating us from our fundamentalist sisters and brothers.

To them we must insist that literal translation is not enough. Scripture must be understood contextually. An episode on *The Twilight Zone* illustrates my point nicely. Visitors come from another planet, and one of them speaks before an assembly of the United Nations, stating that he and his race wish only to serve humankind; they subsequently demonstrate their goodwill by turning earth into paradise. A skeptical official assigns two decoding specialists to interpret a book that the visitor accidentally left on a conference table. In due time the two manage to translate its title — *To Serve Man* — but nothing more. One of the two eventually joins a horde of people who board a spaceship to travel to the visitors' planet, which they have heard is even more wonderful than earth; the other specialist continues her work, at last breaking the code. Desperately, but too late, she runs to the launching pad and yells, "Come back; it's a cookbook!" The rest of us will take no pleasure in seeing the obscenity of Christian brothers and sisters, particularly television evangelists, devouring one another. But we must not judge all evangelicals by power-hungry television evangelists.

Whereas the intolerance of evangelicals leads to cannibalism, the threat to those of our persuasion is that we lose touch with the pulse of faith, its passion and its mystery. To evangelicals we must concede that religious experience is far more complex than ours alone. Then we may even grant that Peter's wild claims make more sense of reality than our sober denials. There is power in both witnesses: Jesus lives, and we are born anew.

A Living Tradition

Deuteronomy 30:15-20; 1 Corinthians 2:6-13;
Matthew 5:17-37

Scripture has the remarkable capacity to surprise those who are nurtured by it day after day. Take the selections we have heard this morning. They shatter to bits the lens through which we are accustomed to viewing the law, one fashioned largely by the Apostle Paul and Martin Luther. For them the Mosaic legislation was a heavy burden imposed on human subjects by its guardians, a load so great that none could bear it without divine assistance. That help came in Jesus of Nazareth, who removed the heavy load and replaced it with an easy yoke and a light burden: "Come unto me, all who labor and are heavy laden. Take my yoke upon you and learn of me. For my yoke is easy, and my burden light."

That is not the impression one gets from reading Deuteronomy 30 and Matthew 5. Quite the contrary! The first lawgiver assures Israel that the teaching is near, in their hearts and within their mouths, and hence can easily be kept. The second lawgiver punctuates his Sermon on the Mount with rigorous demands that virtually nobody can meet: never allow anger to govern your actions, do not lust, don't divorce your spouse, avoid taking oaths, be more righteous than the best Pharisee in the land (which is no mean achievement).

Such straightforward language can hardly be misunderstood, so we are tempted to discard altogether that earlier view on which we cut our teeth. But not entirely, for we also recall two complicating features of biblical history. One, the long story of Israel's failure to abide by the law as made known through Moses, and two, the astonishing freedom that Jesus demonstrated in matters like Sabbath observance and ritual in general. If ancient Israel failed to keep the Mosaic law and hence missed out on the promised good fortune while Jesus and his immediate followers dared to lighten the load in significant ways but did not dispose of it entirely, it therefore follows that the old view which we were about to abandon is not entirely false.

What then shall we do? Scripture corrects our preconceived notions about the old and the new, and yet other Scripture informed that preunderstanding. A possible response to the dilemma in which we find ourselves is to soar to lofty heights far above such ambiguities. That is what Paul is represented as doing in 1 Corinthians 2, for the answer is hidden in esoteric knowledge. By this means only a chosen few grasp the truth, while ordinary believers, like obedient cattle, graze contentedly. Such a resolution to the problem cannot satisfy anyone who reads the larger context of Moses' final sermon to Israel. In Deuteronomy 29:29 [28] he warns against esoteric knowledge: "The hidden things belong to the Lord our God; but the things that are revealed belong to us and to our children forever, that we may keep all the stipulations of this law."

Surely we must pursue another path than that which early gnostics blazed. Perhaps a clue is found within Moses' exhortation to the people: "Choose life, that you and your descendants may live." The decisive factor is a community of faith. The believer alone cannot function as normative, not even a whole generation of such, for one's descendants must be taken into account. In a word, past, present, and future come together when God's promise enters the picture. Precisely what does this imply? Nothing less than that Scripture is a living tradition, one that changes to accommodate the needs of each successive generation. To coin a phrase: Scripture was made for women and men, and not the other way around.

How does this clue help us to understand the problem we have posed? If we consider the two settings of Deuteronomy 30, the answer becomes clear. The imagined context is that of the great lawgiver preaching a final sermon to those whom he led out of

Egyptian bondage. But everyone knows that these listeners and their descendants did not find God's law easy to heed, and they suffered for it. Or at least that is what we read in their own recorded history, one that endeavored to justify God's treatment of these people. The other context is that of an exiled nation, a people whose shoulders are stooped because of the heavy burden of Babylonian captivity. These people have lost their reason for praise and feel the heavy weight of their parents' sins. Now they hear a fresh word, uttered as it were by Moses himself, assuring them that they hold their destiny in their own hands. No longer must they suffer for something over which they had no control. From this day forward their own actions will shape their future for good or ill. A defeated nation is hardly prepared to be told that God's demands are too hard for them. Rather, the word these people waited to hear was a comforting one: "You can do it, for your sake and for those who will come after you."

What is going on here? The author wipes out seven centuries of history and brings together the family of God's people past and present. Their choices become our decisions, just as our actions will someday flow into the lives of those who succeed us. In *Encounters with Silence* Karl Rahner uses an unforgettable image, that of the people of God comprising a long column. Now and then someone drops out and takes along a part of my heart. Another joins the line, but not in my little row. Sooner or later that increasingly shorter row vanishes forever, leaving only the memory of its presence. The total character of that column is shaped by the actions of those who went before, but each stage represents a different entity. Scripture changes accordingly.

If this principle is correct, there is even a place in this column for the one who opted for esoteric wisdom. Therefore, while Moses and Jesus warm their hands by the sacred fire, we must be careful not to leave Paul outside to catch pneumonia. After all, the apostle does quote a partial prophetic word from the latter part of Isaiah. That preserved bit of wisdom is wondrous indeed, for it affirms ultimate mystery. What God has in store for us is indescribable; it stretches the imagination beyond its outermost limits.

From of old no one has heard
    or perceived by the ear,
No eye has seen a God besides thee,
    who works for those who wait for him.

Is it not true? You alone know the hope that fans the flame within your heart, but who would dare deny its ardor? For some of you today, cleaving to God is easy. For others, it is nearly impossible, and for still others, sheer mystery. The household of God consists of them all: those for whom faith is as natural as breathing, and those who gasp for breath, fighting all the while to keep from falling into the abyss. Of course we would choose life. Most of all, however, we ask for a sense of divine presence. That is all, and that is much!

At Ease in Zion

Amos 6:1

Critics of religion are legion, for we practitioners give them ample cause to raise a voice of protest. In many instances, considerable truth resides in the criticism, although religious people are reluctant to acknowledge unpleasant reality. Marx's familiar remark that religion is the opiate of the people cannot be dismissed easily by a church that ignores the plight of the poor and justifies such moral blindness by pointing to the hope of a better life in eternity. The church's claim that spiritual matters far outweigh temporal necessities rings hollow while she stores up earthly treasures for the comfort of her official functionaries, oblivious to widespread misery in society at large. Religious hope conveniently lulls the hungry to sleep, dulling the pain of empty stomachs. Actually, in certain forms of religiosity, physical discomfort is considered evidence of heightened moral virtue, the poor having been God's favorites in some circles for much of the biblical period.

Equally cogent is Freud's well-known dictum that religion represents a child's fantasy, a sort of wish fulfillment that secures one from the harsh realities of adult existence. Belief in God, according to his view, resembles a child's way of reckoning with the world. Rather than facing the cold universe and achieving the emotional maturity expected of adults, many religious people remain frozen in a "child's mentality." This peculiar phenomenon often accompanies stellar intellectual achievements in disciplines other than religion, particularly scientific ones, when an individual freezes religious growth at an infantile stage. Such people never examine their religion with the same rigor they apply to everything else in their lives, so fragile is their sacred canopy.

Feuerbach's devastating observation that human vulnerability generated belief in God implies that our need for security in a hostile universe preceded religion. In other words, human beings invented a powerful Being precisely because they felt helpless and alone. Augustine's oft-cited comment that "Our hearts are restless until they find rest in Thee [God]," viewed from Feuerbach's perspective, suggests that human dis-ease concocted its own remedy, one akin to the false and heartless quip that there are no atheists in a foxhole, or, to update it, in a cancer ward. Projecting our wishes onto the heavens and then bringing them down to earth in flesh and blood amounts to an ingenious ploy — if such it is.

Although these criticisms contain a germ of truth, this correct intuition does not make them wholly reliable, for each critic spoke about what may be called, for want of a better term, popular religion. All of us know that a few representatives of religion have worked diligently to feed the hungry, clothe the naked, and visit the sick and imprisoned, and by doing so have tried to establish God's reign on earth. Some religious people have looked reality squarely in the face without flinching, growing into adulthood in all aspects of life. Moreover, rare individuals have demonstrated amazing capacity to walk with God through the shadow of death — indeed, to retain their faith with no assurance that they will receive a reward either in this life or in the next. It follows that critics of religion have made a valuable contribution by keeping us honest, but they have not spoken the final word. For that we need to turn to religious critics, with the emphasis on the adjective "religious."

In some ways the voice of religious critics is the more devastating of the two, for insiders have the advantage of familiarity. They tell us what we already suspected — that religious people generally think God exists for their benefit, a notion painfully obvious during war. When engaged in battle, every nation claims divine sanction for its actions, in this respect following dubious biblical precedent. To some degree, religious ritual functions magically in the church, giving the impression that human beings control God. Even indications of divine displeasure are viewed as discipline by a loving parent, thus absorbing violence into the sacred. We seem drawn to the notion that suffering, denial, and deprivation make one godly, which stands in considerable tension with the biblical idea that the Creator took pleasure in the universe, pronouncing the finished world extraordinarily good.

When religious people begin to take their ease in Zion, prophetic voices interrupt their drunken stupor. The comfortably placed do not welcome such disturbers of their sleep. The prophet Amos personally experienced the wrath of religious authority, which actually spoke on behalf of the secular state. The priest Amaziah reminded Amos that the temple belonged to the king, whereupon Amos declared that his prophetic denunciation had a higher authority. He has not sought the office of spokesman for God, but he has been summoned, as if by a roaring lion, and he cannot resist. Divine constraint alone fueled the fire that rages within the prophet's soul. Amos's wake-up call makes the censure of the critics of religion appear tame by comparison. How so?

Using flattery and rhetorical flourish, Amos gains the rapt attention of his audience, who understand the ritual being evoked as declaration of destruction on their foes. Every surrounding nation is denounced for atrocities in battle, none of which touched Israel. That fact alone should alert the more astute ones in the audience that the speech does not bode well for them. If these nations are held accountable for acts devoid of human decency, one can be sure that Israelites cannot sell the poor for a pittance and violate the purity of young women with impunity.

In their pride, these people boast that God delivered them from Egyptian bondage, but Amos insists that the same deliverer led their most belligerent enemies from their own captivities into freedom alongside Israel. God's alien work included a much broader plan than Amos's audience recognized, a mysterious enabling of Syria and Philistia, forces that regularly humiliate the chosen people. Furthermore, Israel has indeed been chosen, but that election entails service and responsibility rather than privilege. In Amos's words, "You only have I known of all the families of the earth; therefore I will punish you for all your iniquities."

Religious memory functions to strengthen allegiance, often by means of long recitation of God's saving deeds. With these in mind, Amos constructs his own liturgy of wasted opportunity, asserting that God has sent calamity again and again — famine, drought, pestilence, warfare, earthquake, fire — and yet the people have not changed in any way. After each reference to a particular calamity, the prophet adds a solemn refrain: "Yet you did not return to me." Similarly, either Amos or a later editor borrows a hymn about God's power in nature and adapts its content to function as a doxology of judgment, a willing acknowledgment by a doomed people that its executor has acted justly.

It seems that religious people think God enjoys ritual as much as they do. In eighth-century Israel's case, the celebrative occasions of worship draw large crowds of eager people. Amos throws cold water on their ceremony, taunting them with the startling idea that by coming to the worship centers they actually multiply their offenses against God. The prophet goes so far as to question divine sanction for sacrifice and to label their activities a stench in God's nostrils. Far more important than religious ceremony, Amos argues, is humane treatment of marginalized persons in society.

The era in which Amos burst on the scene was immensely prosperous for Israel's economy, although such prosperity came at the expense of many citizens who grew poorer by the minute. The power of the state also seemed assured, for Israel had defeated its enemies in a few minor skirmishes. Blowing these victories out of proportion, the victorious Israelites boast about their success. Amos knows better, warning against overconfidence and predicting decimation of the population at the hands of an awesome enemy. The destruction will be virtually total, so that a lone survivor will hesitate to speak lest God hear and complete the devastation. While announcing destruction, Amos uses hallowed expressions for divine solicitude — "I will pass through your midst" and "the eyes of the Lord are upon you" — but he understands them as indications of divine fury.

At the heart of all religion lies an element of hope. At times that optimism achieves focused expression; in Amos's day it takes the form of the day of the Lord, which the people long for as God's token of loyalty. The prophet Amos dismisses this hope with a flick of the hand, insisting that the day will be one of darkness and gloom. Sometimes spiritual acts, such as the taking of oaths, can blow up in people's faces. Amos observes that oaths of loyalty, even to ancient deities, will count for nothing, despite their origin in youthful hearts. He announces instead a terrible famine, the departure of oracular inspiration. In short, God will become silent. Both word and vision will vanish, and, devoid of a word from the Source of Life, the people will perish. Such is the prophetic "no" uttered to a people at ease in Jerusalem.

We Christians could ignore Amos's wake-up call if it did not apply to us in intimate detail, for the church has repeated Israel's sins almost to the letter. We boast that our way of salvation is unique, forgetting that God works in countless ways among the race of men and women. We think of ourselves as the chosen people equal to if not superior to the Jews, without a sense of responsibility at all. We recite the Apostles' Creed but give minimal thought to the countless ways our religious claims fail to accord with reality. We have used religion to bash others in more instances than we wish to admit, and we come to worship without allowing our faith to transform our entire lives. We trust in God's protection although we do not acknowledge that our enemies also claim loyalty to the same God. We refuse to acknowledge that divine wrath may possibly differ from our own, and we use religious clichés, oblivious to their potency. We long for the return of Christ, although that event will scarcely result in the bliss we anticipate, given the way we have failed to follow Jesus' example. In light of our own conduct, the prophetic wake-up call suddenly sounds more ominous than we had otherwise imagined.

Prophetic preaching does not divest people of all hope, however, for it holds out a hint of sunshine, a tiny glimmer of light. Seek good and not evil, life as opposed to death, God rather than false gods. It may be that God will have compassion on a repentant few. Here is the prophetic "perhaps." Such preaching protects divine freedom — hence its claim to authenticity. It also values human beings, all of them under the sun. That, too, is a badge of veracity.

These observations suggest that critics of religion resemble gnats on an elephant, a nuisance but only that, whereas religious critics arouse us from a drunken stupor, calling us to repentance and faithful living. Jesus stood in the prophetic tradition when sounding an alarm to those at ease in Zion during his day. Let us pray that the voice of protest by religious critics will continue to echo through the streets of Jerusalem and in every town where people take religion seriously.

The Wonder-Working God

Judges 13:15-21

O ccasionally a few fortunate individuals are privileged to witness the unfolding of history. I was present in Jerusalem at the dedication of the first synagogue for Reform Judaism in the Holy Land. How vividly I recall that summer day in 1963 when the noted archaeologist Nelson Glueck rolled back the veil that had until that second covered the Torah Scroll. Tears filled his eyes as he grasped the solemnity of the moment and the enormity of the events transpiring before him. His natural flair for the dramatic cannot adequately explain those tears; something more was at work on that historic occasion.

Each of us has a moment when time and eternity coalesce, when we perceive the absolute necessity of knowing who we are. Like the responses of biblical thinkers, our responses to this question of personal identity may vary: we are a little lower than God, or we are but dust and ashes. Plato defined man as a two-legged animal without feathers; Diogenes responded by plucking a chicken and bringing it to the Academy, announcing, "Here is Plato's man." We have observed other futile efforts to identify the essence of women and men by defining them as rational animals, laughing animals, tool-making animals, cooking animals. Or as love machines! Closer to the heart of the matter is Kant's ethical imperative and Abraham Heschel's imperative of wonder. That is, we are creatures subject to a sense of ought and a necessity to recognize mystery at the heart of reality itself.

If we are compelled to stand amazed, we know of two responses.

Wonder terrifies, and awe electrifies. Facing our limits cripples us with fear, anxiety, and dread, but facing the hidden possibilities enlivens us, infusing us with hope and enabling us to walk bravely into the future. Our text illustrates the several ways of coming to terms with God's disclosure of reality. It does so in the lives of three people: a son and his parents.

First, the remarkable son, Samson. To this second-generation believer, religion was hearsay, having little impact on his life. So he searched for meaning in the arms of Philistine women. Samson had lost the capacity to be amazed. His remarkable strength gave him the illusion of mastery of every situation. But circumstances forced him to recognize his need for help from one stronger than he. Driven against the wall, he cried for assistance. Twice Samson recovered a sense of wonder. Once God gave him water, the symbol of life. The other time God granted death. Divine mystery — in this instance, remembrance and mercy — overwhelmed the blind second-generation believer. He became one who was forever silenced in God's presence.

Samson, and thousands like him, weighed heavily on the conscience of ancient Israel. The author of Deuteronomy urges again and again that she teach her sons and daughters the meaning of sacred moments, and that she talk about them unceasingly. How her children must have thrilled at the stories of Jericho's fall, Goliath's defeat, and Pharaoh's shame, for rehearsal of God's mighty deeds characterized her faith. Yet in such storytelling lay the dangers of trivializing the holy and of making such events ordinary! Both gave birth to skepticism, in that such occasions rarely, if ever, occurred in the lifetime of believers.

What about Samson's father and mother? For Manoah, divine disclosure was firsthand — and terrifying. When eternity entered time, and time stood still, he fell upon his face and awaited death. The husband of a barren wife, he refused to take her word for mystery but prayed for special corroboration, for personal validation. Like the ancient Jewish historian Josephus, we can only speculate about his motives; perhaps he felt left out and believed that his male dominance was threatened. In any event, the angel rebuked him.

Undaunted, Manoah asked impertinent questions, persisting until he received a clue about life's greatest mystery, the essence of God. Manoah seized the clue and worshipped God as the Wonder Worker. At that moment God rolled back the curtain, and the angel slowly ascended to heaven. Manoah then fell in the other direction and spoke rashly about dying. This awestruck father hardly knew the virtue of silence.

Did Samson's mother fare any better in her encounter with mystery? Barren, the bearer of God's burden, she remained silent in her affliction and was visited by the angel, who promised the birth of a wondrous son. She believed his word and intuited his identity. Furthermore, she exercised extraordinary restraint and did not ask for information beyond what God's messenger volunteered. She divulged all to her husband, and later ran for him to include him in a special moment of divine disclosure, standing aside and letting her husband enjoy the spotlight from that moment forward. When God entered time, she watched in awe, then fell upon her knees. For her the mystery was enlivening, enabling her to assure her husband, "We shall not die." No power can deny me the son promised by the angel, she thought, for in her view the God who works wonders brings life, not death.

*   *   *

In each of us rests a little bit of each biblical character. At times we act like second-generation Christians who have never brushed against mystery. Our lives are wholly ordinary, characterized by trivia, devoid of Transcendence, wholly this-worldly. Thus we cannot confirm the truth of what our ancestors have affirmed. At other times we face mystery with sheer terror, for we know our frame. Like Isaiah, we cry out that we are going to die, since we have seen the true King. On rare occasions we dare to stare God in the face, confident that death is not the final word.

I cannot claim to know when and where each of you comes face to face with God. For some of us the curtain rolls back when death and its manifestations stare us in the face. Others see into eternity when looking into the soul of another creature made in God's image. Still others of us meet God when alone or when nature transforms itself before our very eyes.

Regardless of the occasion, I can only say that individuals are fortunate indeed to be looking when God unveils the curtain of eternity for a moment. Then we hear the wife of Manoah catch her breath and affirm life. In the end, like Job, we are reduced to silence as we exclaim with him, "I had heard of thee secondhand. Now my eyes behold thee, and I repent [in] dust and ashes." Enlivened, purified, we stand with grateful hearts as the heavenly chorus bursts into singing one exhilarating word: "Glory!"

Powerful forces seek to erase the memory of these encounters with divine mystery. Although the tears may flow unashamedly, we can still give vent to wonder, confident that no power on earth can erase either the memory or the anticipation of the vision of God.

I Set Before You Life and Death

Deuteronomy 30:15-20

From time immemorial, the New Year has cast a powerful spell over the human imagination. Ancient peoples surrounded it with diverse ceremonial occasions, from enactment of creation to celebration of the king's marriage with the representative of God's holy priestesses. The turn of the year constituted a return to the beginning of things, threatening a return of chaos, disorder, darkness. The many solemn religious rituals endeavored to secure order, well-being, and divine favor in this highly propitious hour. Anxiously but hopefully, the people waited for signs that the new beginning promised blessing, peace, and stability for one and all. In ancient Israel, the New Year seems to have prompted the covenant community to renew her commitment to God and the divine will. Such reappraisal of one's daily life and inner disposition gave voice to eager expectation. The new year stood before God's people, a door of hope. She had only to open that door and enter the land of promise and plenty.

For us, too, the coming of the New Year holds incredible promise but conceals a tiny measure of terror over the unknown. Those of us who linger before the television set on New Year's Eve witness a modern ritual at Times Square and join the singing of "Auld Lang Syne." Young and old journey to Times Square, braving the elements, just to participate in the momentary ecstasy of the coming of a new year. Close-ups seem — to my eyes, at least — to catch a glimpse of combined feelings of hope and anxiety. We stand at the threshold of a new era, and we do not know whether to rejoice freely or to quake in our boots.

Fortunately, renewal occurs in some circles at times other than those governed by a calendar. Perhaps one of the most beautiful features of academic life is the beginning of new semesters. The slate is wiped clean, and we begin anew from scratch. Judgments come and go, and we have time to profit from them, knowing precisely where we stand.

Our common religious life enjoys many such new beginnings. The power of forgiveness drives our sins into oblivion, so that we need not remember them any more. All our petty, little, base deeds and words are blotted out of God's memory, and we are cleansed whiter than snow. As a result, we begin anew in our many relationships (in marriage, in relating to our children or parents, in dealing with friends and acquaintances). Fresh possibilities electrify as we renew our vows before God and one another. Habits are broken, and new ones begin to form. Nothing approaches the power of forgiveness in transforming life itself.

The text envisions a new beginning in ancient Israel, one totally unconnected to a new year. The speaker for the Lord blots out six centuries of human history and urges Israel to start over once again as if those fruitless years had never occurred. To be sure, sacred memory played a minor role in those centuries between Moses and Josiah. All had not been shameful acts of reprobation. But the sum total of Israel's history was a big zero. It amounted to an aborted birth: Israel rebelled, pursued Canaanite gods, oppressed the poor and defenseless, and misplaced priorities. Only by such a reading of her history could she discover a reason for the present curses under which she dwelt. Exiled from her land, driven into captivity away from God, she sought her Lord in vain.

The spokesman for God promises renewed hope, for God stands ready to forgive. Sin has not ruined God's compassion, but in abounding love God turns to Israel with an offer of life. In a sense, we have here a summary of everything God asks of us creatures. The message is so simple that a little child can understand it, even if the language is extraordinarily abstract for the Bible.

God offers the people a choice and demands a response. No one can avoid making a fateful decision. "Behold, I set before you this day life and death. Choose life!" To explain the force of this offer, the speaker extends the scope of the terms for the highest good and the greatest dread. What is life? He explains that it is good, while death is evil. Life stands for blessing; death, for God's curse. Astonishingly, the speaker deems it necessary to endorse life as the correct choice. In Israel, suicide was rarely chosen, and then only as a result of unbearable shame or intense loyalty to a fallen hero. Only Job and Ecclesiastes truly desire death, and they have mixed feelings about it. Two prophets, Elijah and Jonah, express a death wish, too, but theirs amounts to self-pity.

Everyone knew that life, blessing, the good was no vague abstraction, despite the language. "He has shown you, O mortal, what is good, and what does the Lord require of you but to do justice, to love mercy, and to walk humbly with your God?" This is how Micah defined the weighty word "good." Our speaker does not leave the content a mystery, for he specifies the various components of life, blessing, and the good.

These words describe the result of obedience to God, which is itself a rich concept. It consists of love — that is, the disposition of the heart and walking in God's way, or external conduct — and keeping the divine commandments, or constancy in relationship. Life, therefore, consists of a loving heart, exemplary conduct, and trustworthiness in all circumstances. God's blessing thus consists of a quality of relationship, not the length of days granted us or the trappings of wealth and divine favor. Life, blessing, the good — these expressions describe God's presence with us. God is life, blessing, the good. Having recognized this, we shall live, multiply, and dwell securely in the land.

The speaker perceives a hidden danger lurking behind the door of each Israelite. Like Cain, who was admonished to master the wild beast crouched in readiness to strike him, Israel is warned that she can indeed turn away, refuse to hear, and bow down before alien gods. Should she fail to conquer this enemy, she will perish in God's promised land, so close, and yet so far away. Fully convinced of this danger, the speaker makes a solemn promise: I declare to you this very day that you will perish without hope. In modern parlance, Israel becomes a terminal patient!

Confronted with a choice, Israel now listens to a dreadful oath in which heaven and earth are summoned as witnesses. Her decision is fraught with consequence, since God has sworn before witnesses. Choose life. Now we hear the affectionate language of lovers and parents: love, obey, cleave to the Lord.

Given the context in which we live, we hear these emphases on space and time with fresh power today. The will of God is not far off, so that you would have to search for it in high heaven or beyond the sea. Instead, it confronts you as a gift, very near to you. Life is present, in your heart, and you can keep God's commands. Furthermore, past, present, and future coalesce in this moment. The land that God swore to give to Israel in the past can be reclaimed this day for you and your descendants for years to come.

We notice one jarring note in this text. The speaker purports to be Moses. Now we know that Moses was not given any second chance. Thus we cannot seize the gift without recognizing the mystery of God's free choice. The Lord sets life and death before us as sheer grace. But at the same time, by our decision we control in some measure its quality and length. So the text joins together human responsibility and divine sovereignty in marvelous fashion. We seize the gift of life, only to discover that God offers the divine self. Like Job, we marvel at the wondrous mystery unfolding before our very eyes, for we have been created anew.

MEDITATIONS

Psalm 8

Psalms is often called the hymnal of the postexilic period (after the return to Judah in 538 and the rebuilding of the temple, completed in 516 B.C.E.). The individual psalms constitute the daily worship of that era, but many of the hymns, prayers, and laments may well contain much older traditions. Because of the conservative nature of worship and the universal or timeless sentiments, one rarely finds adequate means of establishing a date of a specific psalm or of placing it in a particular social context. Psalm 8 is a meditation issuing in wonder and praise. Such meditations are intentionally didactic — that is, they aim to teach. Hence the use of a literary device known as *inclusio,* the refrain that introduces and concludes the psalm (vv. 1 and 9).

The first verse extols the divine name, for which there is ample precedent in Deuteronomy, which presents a theology of the Lord's name. The name is personified and actually represents God: "I will put my name in [Shechem]" means the virtual presence of God at the sacred shrine. Glory functions similarly in some texts. Verses 1-2 observe that praise is instinctive, issuing from speechless infants. Another psalm, 19, attributes celestial praise of the Lord to the heavens themselves. One thinks also of Jesus' remark about truth on the lips of children. According to Proverbs 8:22-36, the final creative act prompts praise from Wisdom, God's companion, and Job 38:7 speaks of songs breaking out among the morning stars and divine beings. Our sense of wonder when we behold the mystery of creation has important precedent! Verse 2 informs us that the psalmist whose eyes misted in worship was also a realist. Evil exists out there. Nevertheless, the psalmist recognizes its limits, noting that God imposed a bulwark to keep evil at a distance. The fourth through eighth verses zero in on the status of human beings in this majestic universe. Here it is said that they exercise royal prerogative, as Genesis 1:26 suggests: they are just below God, are crowned with honor, and rule all creatures. This high view was not shared by all biblical writers. Job 41 names a sea creature — Leviathan, or cosmic evil — who resists human domination and can be subdued by God alone. Job 7:17-21 seems to be a parody of Psalm 8, for Job complains because God remembers him and won't look away so he can find relief in death. Psalm 144:3-4 answers the question "What are mortals?" quite differently from Psalm 8. They are mere breath, passing shadows! Ecclesiastes fully concurred in this view.

Psalm 30

This psalm is a thanksgiving hymn. It presupposes a situation of great distress that has now been removed. The psalmist thinks of emerging from Sheol, a *symbol* for extreme suffering. Like the Mesopotamians, who spoke of the underworld as a land of no return, the Israelites believed that anyone who actually entered Sheol quickly faded into shadowy existence. Sickness was believed to place one under Sheol's power, but one could emerge from such "partial" residence in that domain. Verse 2 describes the Lord as attentive and a healer, recalling the divine word to Moses in connection with the deliverance from Egypt (Exod. 15:26; note that the Lord claims to be a *warrior* in his dealings with some, and a *healer* in his dealings with others). A grateful psalmist urges others to praise God, whose momentary anger is dwarfed by lasting favor (vv. 4-5). This point is made in an unforgettable story about the Lord's self-manifestation to Moses, who wishes to see God (Exod. 34:6-7). Later worshippers often cite the merciful attributes of the Lord when seeking deliverance from adversity. The fifth verse affirms that weeping, like divine anger, disappears with the light of day. In verses 6-7 the psalmist ponders the way sin came to expression as a result of overconfidence. The Lord who generously bestowed things we treasure also took them away. This is the lesson Job also learned. Like Psalm 88, this one asks God what profit results from a worshipper's sojourn in Sheol. Verse 9 poses a rhetorical question whose answer is well known. "Will the dust of a corpse praise the Lord?" Of course not! Once again a psalmist appeals to divine vanity, or possibly to something deeper — the threat to God's very existence. The reasoning is clear and forceful, and later rabbis (and survivors of the Holocaust) frequently resort to it. If worshippers vanish, then God also disappears! Therefore God depends on Israel for life, just as Israel relies on the Lord. Perhaps the argument is flawed, but its power cannot be denied. Then comes an appeal to be heard and to be helped; the language for "helper" is the same with respect to woman in Genesis 2:18 ("I will make Adam a helper"). Verses 11-12 report that the prayer achieved its goal. Deliverance becomes a reality.

Psalm 39

This psalm is a reflective lament, a complaint to God that has a high degree of self-examination. In the initial verse the psalmist perceives that speech or its absence can mask one's true character and that expressed thoughts are actually more dangerous than silence. The point is borne out in the history of Joban interpretation. Although the narrator reports that the afflicted Job did not sin with his lips, later rabbinic interpreters pointed out that his heart was a different matter. Because silence in the presence of misconduct can be interpreted as approval, the psalmist risked being classified as one of the villains. Verse 3 implies that the psalmist's actual offense, which resulted from anger, was an expression of envy, like the feeling articulated in detail by the author of Psalm 73. Seeing wicked people prosper is never easy for religious individuals, for something seems to be wrong with the world itself. The psalmist did the right thing — resorted to prayer (v. 4), asking for a status report. "How long will I live?" Here the psalmist uses a Hebrew word for an expression of the final outpouring of divine fury, a word used by Amos with reference to the destruction of Israel ("The *end* has come on my people Israel"). Verse 5 concedes that mortals vanish quickly like breath, like shadows. The resemblance to Ecclesiastes is striking, as is the mournful reminder in verse 6 that we strive to acquire things with no knowledge of who will enjoy them. One recalls Jesus' sharp rebuke of the rich fool who amassed a fortune only to hear the dreaded announcement, "This night your soul will be required of you." In verse 7 the psalmist makes the right move, resolving to trust in God. Job could muster no such hope. Trust, however, removes reproach. No one likes to serve as an occasion for mockery, as Joel 2:26-27 demonstrates. God's educative chastening still hurts (v. 10), and the psalmist pleads for respite before all treasures vanish. Verse 12 compares the psalmist to revered ancestors, sojourners on earth. A pun occurs here on the name "Hebrews," which means "those who cross over, wanderers." The final request in verse 13 is puzzling. It seems to say, "Leave me alone so I can have some peace before I die," which corresponds to Job's plea in Job 14:6. The verb may mean "Rescue me," which fits the context better.

*   *   *

Life's brevity provokes this psalmist to cry out for quality existence during the short time between womb and tomb. Certain adversaries, determined to prevent such abundant living, seemed ever present, but an even greater obstacle loomed before the author: God's delayed response to eager anticipation. Two images stand over against one another: sinners confronting the psalmist, and the psalmist standing before God, *coram deo.* Desiring to escape the former confrontation and to tarry in the divine relationship, this individual determines to gain complete mastery over speech, for which the image of a bridle or muzzle is used. The psalmist intends to suppress speech, thereby assuring that nothing unworthy issues from his lips. This noble sentiment later occurs within a prayer preserved in Sirach 22:27–23:6: "O that a guard were set over my mouth, and a seal of prudence upon my lips, that it may keep me from falling, so that my tongue may not destroy me!" (v. 27).

Anxiety over the ephemerality of existence overcame this determination to keep quiet, however, issuing in a poignant request directed at God: "Tell me how long I have to live." The psalmist realizes that God utters the decisive word about the length of our life on earth, one that is all too short. Whereas the author of Psalm 19 thought of the whole universe proclaiming God's praise without benefit of words, this troubled worshipper focuses on the transient and futile character of life, using a pregnant word, *hebel,* that functions as the thematic utterance at the center of the book of Ecclesiastes. Indeed, both Psalm 39 and Ecclesiastes link the concept of futility with the notion of a shadow, indicating something insubstantial. Like the author of Ecclesiastes, the psalmist comes very close to despair.

A fundamental transition takes place in verse 7 (v. 8 in Hebrew) with the expression "and now." The psalmist complains that God keeps him waiting, which is particularly vexing in light of life's brevity. Perhaps the real source of dismay derives from something else, the thought of being denied divine presence at all. The psalmist draws this conclusion from the fact that God currently administers harsh punishment on a frail earth creature whose days are already numbered. Like the prophet Hosea, the psalmist perceives God as destructive, using the image of a moth devouring cloth. The irony inherent in this simile enhances the terror before a punishing god, for the life span of moths is even shorter than that of human beings. Appealing to divine compassion, the psalmist pleads for a more favorable hearing, one usually offered to sojourners, who enjoyed special protection under a code of hospitality for persons just passing through. The same argument occurs in a liturgy recorded in Jeremiah 14:1–15:2 (especially vv. 8-9); this text also proclaims the Lord as source of hope (v. 22). Life is a short journey, the psalmist realizes, one that links all generations.

This recognition that the ancestors have sojourned on earth only temporarily prompts the psalmist to make an audacious request, one familiar to those who know about Job's agonizing cry — that God look away for a moment so that he might experience joy before passing into oblivion. The psalm ends with thoughts about utter silence, the tongue having been stilled by the most effective muzzle of all, death.

Psalm 82

In the ancient Near East, royal ideology depicted rulers as champions of widows, orphans, and strangers in the land. Any king who failed to look after the needs of the powerless within his empire was derelict in duty and could be asked to relinquish the throne, to step down in favor of a more compassionate successor. Psalm 82 projects this ideal on the heavens, on the principle of the lesser to the greater. The argument assumes a polytheistic environment, with a single God — in this instance, Elohim — confronting the rest of the deities and accusing them of failing to carry out their responsibilities with respect to weak and defenseless members of society. The idea of a divine council, perhaps modeled on earthly courts of power, finds echo in a few biblical texts, specifically the artfully conceived story about Micaiah ben Imlah in 1 Kings 22, and also in the powerful description of Isaiah's call in chapter 6 and the Prologue to the book of Job.

The accusing God, having taken a seat in judgment, uses human language of intense affliction: "How long?" Injustice reigns, like the gods themselves, as they favor persons offering bribes and consequently deny justice to individuals lacking resources. The accusation heaps up adjectives for the weakest citizens, persons without parents and defenders. The speaker accuses the gods, presumably, of lacking knowledge and understanding, and thus of walking around in total darkness so that the very foundations of the earth are shaken. Behind this moral sense of darkness rests the idea that the Creator founded earth on righteousness, an act that is being seriously undermined by the gods themselves.

A change of speakers is signaled in verse 8, as the psalmist pleads with God to stand up and execute justice. The same sentiment, now stated in prophetic prediction, occurs in Joel 3:12, which has the Lord entering into judgment against all nations. Who is the speaker in verses 6-7 of this psalm? The first-person pronoun occurs without further identification. The implied speaker is God, who continues the accusation against the other deities, reminding them of their mortality. This astonishing remark represents ancient Israel's attitude to religious pantheons. Although granting the existence of other gods, the psalmist and those he addressed made a decisive distinction between their God and all the others. This difference best surfaces in the title "the living God," whereas the other gods died like human beings, even princes among men and women. This assurance that the champion of the weak alone survives death's ravages must have brought immense comfort to troubled victims of society.

Psalm 88

Psalm 88 is an unrelieved lament, one that uses the idea of being forgotten to characterize both the worshipper and the object of that adoration. Personal distress convinces the psalmist that Sheol has already claimed its victim (vv. 6-12). The poet has fallen into the Pit and dwells in Sheol, overwhelmed by heavily crashing waves. Readers may think of Jonah's cry from the belly of the great fish (Jonah 2), where this same imagery abounds.

The psalmist has been shunned by the religious community as ritually unclean (that is the sense of "an abomination"). Left alone, the psalmist offers petition to the Wonder Worker, but with a vengeance. A brilliant idea has formed in the midst of discomfort: God is about to lose a devotee! Hence the psalmist's strange argument: "Can you perform awesome deeds after your worshipper dies? Of course not. Do dead people worship you? No! If you like to hear the sounds of praise, you had better rescue me now before my voice is stilled in death." This appeal reaches deeply into the familiar liturgical language of bygone days, heaping together expressions for the Lord's mighty deeds in past generations. I refer to the reference to "wonder," "steadfast love," "faithfulness," and "saving deeds." Numerous cultic recitations in the Bible praise God in such language, but the psalmist reminds the Lord of the perceived discrepancy between the community's confessions of faith and contemporary reality. The psalmist sees no evidence for such redemptive acts, and a nagging suspicion that God has forgotten the victim overwhelms the psalmist. Cries evoke no divine response, unless it is an active game of hide-and-seek (v. 13). Like Job, who also complains bitterly about a hiding God, the psalmist feels buffeted on every side by the Lord. Unfortunately, no relief comes, and the psalm concludes on a jarring note. God separates the psalmist from those friends who might bring a measure of comfort. The unusual expression "lover and friend" stands out like an amaryllis among pansies. Sheol's darkness veils all hint of light.

Psalm 137

In this psalm, a tale of two cities, Jerusalem and Babylon, is held together by a single theme — memory. Enforced residence in Babylonia evokes within the subject Judeans powerful feelings about their former residence. Nostalgia increases as a result of mockery, the captives being compelled to sing a song of Zion just as bound Samson had been ordered to make sport in the midst of Philistines during their religious celebrations. Tears flow down the cheeks of the tormented Judeans as freely as the waters flow in the canals of their new settlement, twice referred to simply as "there." Perhaps, too, the word "Babel" carries an echo of the ancient tradition about God's scattering of the people who attempted to build a tower to heaven, when languages flowed unchecked and unrecognized.

The power of memory exacerbates the captives' situation, prompting an uncooperative response. "How can we sing *the Lord's song* in a strange land?" Whereas the mirth-makers had requested a song of Zion, the Judeans rephrase the request, emphasizing the object of adoration in the songs. The mockers had also mentioned *simḥah,* joy, but the tormented will have none of that. Although they are not free to do as they please, the Judean captives pronounce a curse against themselves if they forget Jerusalem. The imprecation perfectly matches the envisioned offenses. "If I forget Jerusalem and permit my talented hands to play a musical instrument, may my fingers forget their skill, and if my tongue does not remember to keep silent, then may it cleave to my cheek." The curse is artfully formed into an a-b-b-a pattern, a *chiasm.* Structurally, it can be represented as follows:

If I forget Jerusalem: may my right hand forget.
May my tongue cleave to my cheek: *if I do not remember.*

The punishment fits the crime in each instance. This concern for parity extends also to the mention of the two cities. Twice Babylon is mentioned, matching the two references to Zion. The three identifications of Jerusalem as the city of ardor take precedence over the other two, even though Zion and Jerusalem are the same location.

The self-curse encourages tormented Judeans to widen the power of the curse to include Edomites, whose conduct during the fall of Jerusalem to Babylonian soldiers was particularly vexing. Memory thus evinces a vengeful curse against Edom as Babylon-like, a benediction pronounced on anyone who would dash the heads of Edomite infants against rocks. How sweet the thought of revenge to those enduring ridicule and shame! Even the Lord is invited to do some remembering of this infamy at the hands of Edomites. Beneath the surface of this request lies a *quid pro quo* mentality; we have done our part, now you do yours. Suffering encourages this sort of thinking at the same time that it often strengthens character and resolve. Things never turn out to be quite as simple as we wish, even in the one psalm that can be dated definitely as postexilic.

Loving God

When I think about loving God, my thoughts overwhelm me. I barely love people whom I see and touch, whose actions convey their feelings toward me, whether or not I am loved in return. With God none of this is possible. I cannot see the Invisible One, cannot touch the Heaven Dweller, cannot know whether or not my love has any object at all. Even the thought of loving the Holy One terrifies me, for I am flesh and blood. I want to love God, but am afraid the fire will consume me.

The psalmist who wrote the following words struggled with these same issues, resolving them in a flurry of images:

> O Lord, in the heavens — your loving kindness,
>   your faithfulness — up to the clouds.
> Your saving deeds — like mighty mountains,
>   your judgments — the watery deep.
> Both people and animals you rescue, O Lord.
> How precious your loving kindness, O God;
>   mortals take refuge in the shadow of your wings,
>   eating from the abundance of your temple;
>   yes, you even let them drink from your river of delights.
> For with you is a fountain of life,
>   in your light we behold light. (Ps. 36:5-9)

This object of superlative praise took one further step, becoming flesh and blood to bring us together again. O Lord, how precious the very thought of you!

The Controversy over Moderates and Conservatives

Galatians 1:11-24

Modernism is no new phenomenon. Societies have always struggled to strike a balance between preserving past values and remaining open to the future. Like its later Christian counterpart, the Jewish community split over rival teachers, the modernist Hillel and the traditionalist Shammai. The former developed sophisticated rules for understanding Scripture, noting every minor feature, while Shammai relied on ancestral tradition. How did they settle the dispute? By resorting to a voice from heaven, a *Bath Qol*, which declared both Hillel and Shammai to be right but stated that in cases of ethical conduct, *halakah*, Hillel was to be followed. Even so, another story informs us that, Hillel's brilliance notwithstanding, colleagues ignored him until he noted in passing that he learned the value of tradition from his teacher.

That struggle is reconstituted in the Christian community, although we hear only one side. A modernist, Paul, dares to depart from the way as taught by Jesus' disciples, guardians of the tradition. Refusing to take the easy path by appealing to his having met Peter and James, Paul distances himself from them in the strongest language ("Before God, I am not lying"). Hoping to settle the dispute once and for all, he appeals to a heavenly voice. Why did this strategy fail? Because autobiography carries with it an inherent suspicion of self-interest. Bypassing tradition landed him in hot water, and Paul was forced to rely on personal testimony. That move invariably raises the question of reliability. Is he telling the truth?

When we come down to it, personal testimony lies at the heart of the religious life. We can only bear witness to our experience, which necessarily differs from that of others. Personal disposition inclines us toward the authority of the past or the openness of the unfolding present. Conflict is inevitable. So long as our testimony has a humble qualifier — this is my understanding, but I may be wrong! — it lacks persuasive force in some circles. The opposite testimony may carry the day, but so did the forces arrayed against Jesus. Let us therefore humbly concede our ignorance and hope for the dawn of a new day when God puts an end to human rivalries.

The Veiling and Unveiling
of the Holy

I have recently had occasion to reflect seriously on my commitment to theological education. As a consequence, my remarks, though brief, carry heavy conviction. In essence, I wish to describe the mission of the divinity school in two ways that are at first glance mutually contradictory. The task of the divinity school is (1) to destroy every vestige of professionalism surrounding the ministry, and (2) to equip students to function as professionals. What do I mean by these startling comments?

I. To Destroy Every Vestige of Professionalism

As I view it, our primary goal is to communicate the gravity of the task to which divinity students have committed their lives, to make sure that they come up against knowledge of its weightiness at every moment of their ministry. Only the person who trembles before God and others can expect to convince others that he or she realizes the gravity of trafficking in matters holy. Both minister and parishioner stand before God as "beggars," and neither can lay claim to special favor or knowledge. Still, parishioners believe that ministers come in contact with life's ambiguities, and they often expect answers concerning them. Confronted by the necessity of speaking a meaningful word to parents who have just lost a child, to elderly people whose bodies and minds ache without ceasing, to someone betrayed by a beloved, to a person prone to wayward behavior, ministers must speak from experience and conviction. Unless they have wrestled with God and, like Jacob, gained at least a Pyrrhic victory now and again, they can but offer banal platitudes for hearts longing to hear God's promises filled with hope.

Inasmuch as ministers cannot avoid dealing with parishioners in crises, they must know what struggle does to the human psyche. Our task as a divinity school, then, is to insist that students begin to work out their salvation with fear and trembling. They must catch a fleeting glimpse of what it means to be religious — I mean, what belief in God really constitutes. Such a glimpse will emphasize the limits to all knowledge, especially knowledge about God, and will demand absolute honesty in dealing with such matters as grace, sin, life after death, and so forth. By familiarizing students with the traditions they have inherited (biblical, ethical, theological, and historical), the divinity school broadens their vision and enables them to see that they can draw upon the collective experience of religious peoples. Thus they perceive the necessity of carrying the torch a few steps further in the race of life, fully aware of the long line of predecessors who urge us on despite fatigue, uncertainty, and obstacles both apparent and hidden.

In short, the task of the divinity school is to unveil the holy so that all who hope to function as spokespersons of that other world may look into the fire that will rage within their souls from that moment forward. If any student leaves a divinity school without having felt the power of a consuming fire, without having experienced the divine constraint that propels him or her forward in God's service in spite of a desire to remain silent and to seek a less demanding task, we teachers have failed in our singular mission.

II. To Equip Students to Function as Professionals

At the same time that our task is to destroy every vestige of professionalism, we endeavor to equip students to function as professionals. Anyone who has pulled back the curtain and beheld the raging fire knows that we cannot endure the heat of such flames. It is too much for us. Tradition has made much of the destructive power of holiness: in ancient Israel, only three lifted the veil and dared to look upon God. One survived, one died, and another went mad. In effect, no one can bear the weight of the ministry as I have defined it thus far. The burden of representing God in every realm of life, the responsibility of speaking when no word comes, of providing answers when there are none, and of offering hope when such assurances defy reason — such a load is too much for any human being. Hence the necessity of a certain kind of professionalism.

The divinity school must enable its graduates to function as professionals, by which I mean it must help them to be satisfied with partial answers, half-commitments, compromises, and doubting thoughts. Ministers who have looked on the Holy One must learn to live with desert moments, for such fleeting glimpses will be rare. Most of their hours will be spent in drudgery, in seeing that the machine of religion runs as smoothly as possible. Only as ministers gain insight into the necessity of a certain kind of professionalism will they be able to live with themselves during those long droughts. Although they may enter periods when the fiery presence has withdrawn and remains afar off, ministers must carry on as if they have emerged fresh from an encounter with the Holy. Only by developing a powerful memory can they possibly survive the dark night of the soul that befalls most of us. This is what I mean by the necessity of equipping students to function professionally. At the same time, we must alert students to a hidden danger: churches tend to mold ministers into their own images of what a minister should be, viewing them as hired hands. Only as we offer opportunities for students to define their understanding of ministry in the light of what they beheld when the veil was rolled back will they refuse to be refashioned and dominated by earthly fires, however attractive they may be.

In arriving at these conclusions, I have kept ever before me certain biblical texts, chief of which are the calls of Jeremiah and Isaiah. Both prophets looked upon the Holy One and felt the burden as more than they could bear, while at the same time both functioned as God's spokesmen, although consciousness of the dark night of the soul nearly drove them mad. Almost — but not quite — for they derived comfort from the divine promise "I shall be with you."

Our task, as I see it, is to enable students to hear that word anew.

The Common Thread

L ast year I read a book about the history of a little village just outside Cambridge. The title of that book was *A Common Stream*. The author discussed Foxton's emergence in the fourth century when a Roman soldier decided to retire in England, the vicissitudes of a town caught between ethnic and religious wars, its near extinction during the Black Death, the vast changes introduced by hedges that separated one farmer's land from another's, and the erosion of a sense of common land and existence. Although the story of the town constantly shifted to nearby places of power, often religious, the reader never forgot that a common stream ran through the middle of the town. It was to this common stream that everyone turned for vital water, and at this water source they acknowledged that Foxton comprised a community in the deepest sense of the word. To be sure, the drying up of that common stream was viewed as one unwelcome result of progress, and the author longed for the good old days. Perhaps my remarks about the common thread in our curriculum will strike some of you as old-fashioned nostalgia, but what can you expect from one who gets more excited about events and ideas in the ancient world than about contemporary rock music or some forms of modern art?

Just what is the common thread in our curriculum that, like the scarlet rope placed on Rahab's roof, guarantees life to those who recognize its worth? Better still, what is the common stream from which we all drink, students and faculty alike? I confessed to one of my colleagues, Fernando Segovia, that I honestly did not know the answer. He advised me to suggest that it is old age, and then to talk about something that is second nature to me. Having been told on Wednesday that some of my students think that I would make a nice grandfather, I am not quite sure how to interpret my colleague's remark! But it reminds me of a story about a biology professor at Berkeley who was known to have given Ph.D. exams on the subject that he happened to be studying at the time. On one occasion a student paid a custodian to find out what books the professor was reading. The result: books on camels. So the student learned everything about camels. But his exam was on bees. Therefore, the student began the answer in the following manner: "The bee is entirely unlike the camel, which . . ."

But I have put off answering the question long enough. I believe the common stream is the commitment that all of us share to search for what it means to speak on behalf of the living God. Notice that I have defined that common element as something we possess and yet do not possess. Whereas the commitment is ours, the rest is the object of a quest. This commitment points to the eternal Source of our quest, the One who has bestowed on us a vision of a world that has been healed of the broken relationships blighting its landscape today. That vision, however blurred, draws us toward another kingdom, one in which God's will shapes every thought and deed. The gap between the real and the ideal fuels our actions and keeps us humble, for we know that God alone can transform human nature. We act in full awareness that we may never see any results, for the forces of evil will not surrender without resisting valiantly.

As a faculty we aspire to introduce students to the rich resources of religious tradition, enabling them to understand and to appreciate their spiritual pilgrimage. By drawing on this vast store of knowledge, they may then be able to meet parishioners' needs. Having committed themselves to the Living God, ministers may escape the "burnout" that often strikes even the well intentioned. Success is by no means assured, however. Even those who have caught a vision of the spiritual realm and have become citizens of another country may find ordinary ministry to be empty, may long for the chance to return to the authentic fountain.

May I share with you the contents of a recent letter from a graduate of this school? She is now a successful minister, happily married to a rising scholar in his field, well adjusted in every way, but desperately missing the opportunity to expand the mind by taking the search seriously. Her cry continues to echo in my ears: "Help me to keep the quest for truth alive." In other words, she has already realized the ease with which the heart and mind are dulled by daily pursuits, however important they may be. Whatever else she may have learned, that student certainly perceived the common thread in our curriculum. We are engaged in a search for authenticity. Not for who we are as such, but for what it means to give an authentic witness.

I am fully aware that my remarks thus far sound very pious, and perhaps they are just that, and I have finally shown my true colors. But, I assure you, they are not spoken lightly. I truly believe that the commitment to search for the way humans have expressed their religious convictions, and the desire to understand what the modern equivalent would be, together make up the most powerful witness to Transcendence in contemporary society. Nevertheless, our confession is necessarily tinged with ignorance, necessitating an admission that we do not know the final answer. As I see it, this astonishing concession sets us apart from many theological seminaries and religious institutions. We do not claim that the last word has been handed down and that all we must do is accept it. Instead, we are busily engaged in shaping that word. Not arrogantly, or boldly, but with stammering tongue and on bended knee.

To recapitulate, the common thread in what goes on here is a commitment to search for authenticity. Only as we retain a balance between our motive for action and our manner of seeking can we hope to achieve a little success in producing ministers as theologians.

Objectivity and Subjectivity
in Teaching

I want to make six points, all really quite simple. Yet they strike me as worthy conversation starters.

1. No one can actually achieve pure objectivity, for at least three reasons: (a) all interpretation arises from certain assumptions, as Bultmann's famous essay demonstrated cogently; (b) much of what one sees lies behind the eyes, as Confucius recognized; and (c) informed and gifted intellects generate passion. In 1964 I attended my first meeting of the Society of Biblical Literature/American Academy of Religion. One historian there claimed that historians are objective, whereas theologians are biased. Such a claim would be laughable if it did not persist in many departments of religious studies today. Sociologists, folklorists, and phenomenologists often are seduced by the lure of "scientific" interpretation, the goal of universities, despite the fact that the best scientists acknowledge their own faith assumptions — theories (visions). Describing religion without taking its spirit into account is as futile as trying to get a rose to bloom after cutting the roots off the plant. Whoever employs such skepticism is like someone wandering in the desert with a lamp looking for the sun in midday.

2. The other extreme, subjectivity, is equally questionable. We cannot return to pre-Enlightenment thought, S. H. Nasr notwithstanding. He would have us formulate Descartes's conclusion quite differently: *cogitor, ergo est* (I am thought, therefore He is) or *cogitor,*

ergo cogito et sum (I am thought, therefore I think and am). Such epistemology easily glides over into fundamentalism — in Nasr's case, Islamic, but in other circles, Christian. A student once told me that he had direct knowledge of absolute truth that even involved choosing which Scripture verses are inspired. In his words, "Truth is arrogant because it is absolute." As I saw things, his truth was delusion. Can we even think of the "relatively absolute"?

3. A hermeneutic of suspicion is essential, both with regard to objectivity's inevitable skepticism and subjectivity's absolutism. We strive for fairness and humility, not objectivity. Because self-serving knowledge, even in moral causes, is always suspect, we subject our own views to the same standards applied to opposing views.

4. There are three stages of knowledge: description, experience, and internalization. I hear a description of fire; I see it; I am consumed in it! To use Job's experience, "I heard about you, God; now I see you; and I reject and repent concerning dust and ashes." Appropriately, the third stage is ambiguous. Grammar and syntax combine to retain mystery at this level.

5. Advocacy belongs to the third level, and privileged data then enter the picture. On the first two levels things are relatively simple. We describe Plato's thought, or Goethe's, or Chaucer's, and enable students to see clearly and immediately. We do not apologize for passion, because these teachings do not require conversion. Advocacy becomes problematic when ideology surfaces — Marxist, Christian, or whatever. Christianity is quintessentially evangelical, demanding an internalization of a way of life, an ethos that is exclusive and all-embracing. *Intelligo ut credam* (I inquire so that I may believe). But does a university have the right to espouse an ideology? I don't know, but I have my doubts. Yet, one cannot remain neutral where ideology is concerned, and a teacher without ultimate commitments is only half a teacher. An Egyptian proverb says it well: Without love there is no instruction.

6. Applied to my own discipline, this means that I endeavor to describe what actually happened back then or the symbolic/fictive world of Israel, thus enabling students to experience for themselves the religious meaning of that report at various stages of the canon.

I leave the process of internalization to students, for that will be their task of a lifetime. Perhaps there are two circles in the educational process: an inner one and an outer one. By attending to the outer circle, we achieve the descriptive task, but from time to time we enter the inner circle when the ancient voice engages our lives. Then we experience *sapientia* — taste! We weave in and out between then and now, achieving representation and revitalizing tradition. To remain within the inner circle is to sever all links with the present, and possibly also with the past, thus canceling our effectiveness as teachers.

To be sure, even these observations betray a particular intellectual and religious context, and to that extent cannot make any claim to objectivity. Nevertheless, I have endeavored to describe the situation as I see it objectively and dispassionately. Like everyone else, I cannot escape my intellectual ethos.

A Taste of Hell: Believing Oneself
Forsaken by God

These days it is difficult to believe in God. Indeed, our society has become so thoroughly secularized that many people see no need for religion in their lives at all. Whatever role a deity played in the past has been taken over by science, and people place their trust in human ingenuity rather than relying on an invisible and remote divine being. To be sure, they freely admit room for all kinds of faith assumptions, but these have nothing to do with a divine being. For them, all talk about a personal God is nonsense. Perhaps belief in a supreme being was necessary in a previous age, but the concept is obsolete; the sooner we stop deluding ourselves, the better it will be.

Even those who retain remnants of traditional faith must do so against heavy odds. The problem of evil stands as an ever-present warning against easy faith. We may be unwilling to credit absolute truth to Archibald MacLeish's clever way of expressing things in *J.B.* ("If God is God, he is not good; if God is good, he is not God"), but we certainly acknowledge the problem this formulation addresses. Any attribution of both power and goodness to deity is fraught with difficulty, for the most superficial study of reality indicates that virtue struggles for its existence against overwhelming odds. The burden of human suffering weighs heavily on the believer, who must come to terms with the outright contradiction between faith in a moral God and recognition that the universe is blind to human goodness. In the face of universal misery, the unanswered questions

"Why?" and "How long?" cry out for response. So far as we can tell, they are greeted with stony silence.

The Bible complicates matters further, particularly when it falls into unworthy hands. As is well known, the world has suffered too much from extremists who, with Bible in hand, went in search of victims: witches, heretics, homosexuals, slaves. The incredible cruelty that accompanied the initial adoption of a sacred book has spawned murders throughout the centuries, and fanaticism in the name of the Bible is alive and well today. The combination of a closed book and a closed mind is devastating; centuries cannot undo the damage of one person so inclined. But even in capable hands the Bible wields a negative influence wherever it is taken seriously. That impact is not limited to its attitude toward women, which is being clarified more and more in current research, but extends beyond to such issues as jingoism and particularism. Here we strike at the very heart of the biblical message, specifically that Yahweh chose a particular nation from among all the peoples of the world. To be sure, occasional reminders do occur that God elected Israel for service — indeed, that God chose Israel as a light to the nations. Still, the scandal of particularity exists — the claim that the *true* God, *Yahweh,* has revealed *himself* to the *Jews.*

Furthermore, that particularism expresses itself in the way God speaks and acts. In short, Yahweh is frequently depicted as a warrior deity with a bellicose nature. The sensitive reader of the Hebrew Bible must surely discover how pervasive this spirit is, for it seems that God's nostrils burn against someone all the time. Divine anger bares itself *ad nauseum;* such reading becomes barely tolerable by occasional recollection that compassion also belongs to the divine nature. Naturally, the constant descriptions of God as destroyer are accompanied by depictions of humans as sinners through and through. In a sense, this becomes a self-fulfilling prophecy.

The inevitable consequence of this harsh presentation of divine and human character is a tendency of believers to select a canon within the canon. For most Christians, this means a decided preference for the New Testament, since they mistakenly believe love is the essential characteristic of God in it. A single glance at the book of Revelation should convey a different message, for nothing in the Old Testament quite measures up to the divine fury expressed here. Nevertheless, it is significant that the tendency to pick and choose from the Bible results in isolating certain universal themes in the Hebrew Bible. It is precisely here that one also finds the emphasis on love and mercy.

Perhaps this quest for the normative center illuminates yet another path, that on which ancient skeptics traveled. Any genuine search for a legitimate center enables readers to discover the important place of doubt in ancient Israelite society. This significant voice bears eloquent testimony to the fact that religion tends to become obsolete, that its convictions harden and refuse to bend with the times. As a result, only the outer shell of the faith persists, and religious institutions function as museums preserving an important heritage from the past. Skeptics recognize this shell for what it is and refuse to be content with lifeless faith. In their minds they envision a living reality, and the attack they launch against hollow religion becomes their means of restoring vitality to a dead faith. Ironically, persons who subscribe to the shell and mistake it for the real thing also look upon those who wish to save faith as its own worst enemies, forgetting that the Hebrew Bible gave an exalted position to men and women who dared to challenge God and sacred tradition.

To repeat, it is not easy to remain a believer today. Religion has a marginal role to play in our secular society, and one can easily get along without God. As a matter of fact, belief in a supreme being only complicates matters, inasmuch as it necessitates coming up with some reasonable answer to the problem of evil. In addition, the believer must explain away all sorts of extreme behavior by those who view the Bible as divine revelation and come to grips with the narrow perspective represented by particularist claims to truth. One means of doing so is by selecting which parts of the Bible are normative. This search for the center naturally leads to the study of dissent within the Old Testament. It follows that religious doubt is an ancient legitimate tradition, one that is ignored at considerable cost.

For Judaism and Christianity, belief in God has always carried with it a firm conviction that the universe is moral. The basis for this understanding of the created order was the Deity's essential moral nature. Since the Creator was ethical, it stood to reason that the world was also subject to a moral order. The repeated emphasis on the goodness of creation in Genesis 1 and the covenant that God made with Noah to assure order after the threat of the Flood testify to the ancient Israelite assurance that one could rely on the universe. In essence this trust in the created order was simply an expression of trust in its Creator.

Such belief became an occasion for profound soul-searching, for frequent eruption of unexplainable suffering made mockery of cherished convictions, when they did not harden religious convictions into expressions of cruelty. We can recognize both tendencies within the book of Job, where faith in a just order crushes an innocent victim. In the end, Job sacrificed his belief in a universe that operated from discernible moral laws. That hard-won insight would seem to be even more appropriate for modern believers.

The collapse of belief in an ethical deity has ushered in a situation that is characterized by at least three significant facts. The first of these is that the world is not governed by moral laws. There is evidence on every hand that randomness characterizes the good and evil that manifest themselves in society. Qoheleth perceived this fact with remarkable clarity: time and chance happen to everyone, as if playing indiscriminately. Those things that we dread — the cancer germ, the car accident, the bomb — do not distinguish between the good and the bad, but rather work havoc with complete disregard of human worth. We may try to escape their power by good works, and even through prayer we may endeavor to enlist divine assistance in this mighty struggle, but neither attempt will alter the situation in the least. The dreaded evil will strike us and those we love with utter indifference. No moral law will govern the disbursement of suffering, and no ethical deity will guarantee the survival of the universe for the sake of human creatures.

The second consequence of vanishing belief in a moral Creator strikes at the very heart of most religious teaching. Since God is not subject to our idea of morality, we have absolutely no claim on the

Deity. Virtue does not have to be rewarded, nor vice punished. This means that we may spend our entire lifetime in constant struggle to do the ethical thing at all costs, only to be met by divine indifference. The same may be said for the person who devoted every moment to vicious conduct, for there is no assurance that God will act to curb that violence. In fact, the odds are that such malicious persons will thrive in modern society, where greed has almost eclipsed human compassion.

A third fact follows on the heels of this awareness that we cannot count on God to reward goodness and punish wickedness. That is the admission that life is unfair. No one who reflects for a moment on the distribution of wealth, for example, can any longer believe that all are equal, for there is no moral explanation for the fact that athletes and movie stars receive millions of dollars for their services while nurses and teachers barely subsist. Nor can one easily justify the disparity of wealth among the nations of the world, particularly since great wealth is often the direct result of exploitation. To be sure, one can downplay such disturbing facts by keeping the eyes focused on the future beyond this present life. But why should death usher in something entirely different from what we have come to know about the universe? Can we be sure that such hopes are not delusions of grandeur?

In short, we can no longer believe that the universe is subject to moral laws, so that virtue pays and wickedness does not. As a matter of fact, we have absolutely no claim on God, even when we have lived exemplary lives in the midst of great adversity. In a word, life is not fair; although sobering, this acknowledgment is hardly crippling. Life's opposite, death, signals the end insofar as we know, and to think otherwise is to rely on cherished convictions that grew out of a worldview that has collapsed.

What, then, is left for believers in our time? We can take comfort in a personal relationship with God, but that is hard to sustain when all conversation is one-sided. Divine silence is thus a problem of such magnitude that it forces one to ask whether or not things were ever different. Can we today believe that biblical claims to revelation are anything more than human perceptions? How should we treat stories about divine self-manifestation, or deal with expressions such as "Thus has the Lord spoken"? Are all claims within the Bible nothing more than human gropings, the product of stammering tongues and noble aspiration? Even if we answer these questions in a manner that stresses continuity between ancients and moderns, and therefore deny absolute truth to religious claims within the Bible, we can nevertheless appreciate the rare insights into the nature of creaturely existence. Impoverished beyond description is the life devoid of self-understandings achieved by biblical writers. Certain perceptions do not depend on belief in a moral universe sustained by deity. We can still recognize our own finitude, and we can continue to confess faith in one who deserves complete allegiance. But the struggle to conform our wills to God's intentions as we understand them stands under a grim reminder that power belongs to those who seek to thwart the effect of goodness. Whether Jew or Christian, we look to one who willingly submits to suffering, and who consequently knows what we ourselves endure daily.

Now if silence has become a problem, how much more is divine villainy. I explored that issue in *A Whirlpool of Torment*, asking, "How can God turn against faithful servants and submit them to tests that propel them headlong into a whirlpool of torment?" Abraham, Jeremiah, Job, Ecclesiastes, the psalmist — all found to their horror that a life of faithfulness did not guarantee comparable behavior on the Deity's part. I have walked beside these lonely men of faith in the path of God-forsakenness, and I fear that their journey has also become that of many others. That we cannot abandon the Lord is both a testimony to the profundity of sacred memory and a constant source of torment. The taste of hell is bitter indeed.

The Twin Enemies of Faith

In his book entitled *Beyond Tragedy*, Reinhold Niebuhr wrote, "Faith is always imperiled on the one side by despair and on the other side by optimism. Of these twin enemies of faith, optimism is the more dangerous." I have often pondered the implications of this profound observation regarding the essential nature of Christian faith, particularly since so many things tilt me toward the skeptical side of the divine-human relationship. Naturally, Niebuhr's analysis of the situation appeals to me, suggesting as it does that I could choose an even more dangerous option.

How can one make the audacious claim that optimism presents a greater threat to the religious life than despair? Although I do not know what Niebuhr had in mind, I can recognize the danger inherent in fleeing to a "convenient God," to use the phrase of Jonathan Magonet, author of *Form and Meaning: Studies in Literary Techniques in the Book of Jonah*. He observes, "When flight from God [does] not work [in Jonah's experience], there is always flight to God, or to that convenient God who makes no demands beyond those the worshipper can comfortably offer." Perhaps this willingness to rest in comfortable arms oblivious to human hurt appeals to many religious individuals because it allows them to surrender fully without the slightest hint of doubt. Believing that such sacrifice of the intellect is a desirable thing, they commit their entire will to preconceptions about the nature of the religious life. Come what may, nothing can controvert their understanding of God. In a sense, dogma has become frozen, locked in a time zone that secures it against attack from every side. The downside of such belief, however, is its stagnation, for anything alive inevitably grows and changes with the circumstances, whether adverse or favorable. Faith, too, alters with emerging situations as loyal oppositionists challenge teachings that have come down to them in good faith. Biblical understandings of God suggest that human circumstances and responses evoke a change in God's essential character.

Whatever one may say about the power of prayer, whether its effect is limited to the one doing the imploring or its impact reaches to the divine disposition as well, biblical faith underscores the remarkable change in God's manner of dealing with human beings as a result of prophetic mediation. These individuals who call on the name of the Lord, which seems to be the original meaning of the popular term *nabi'*, stand in the breach for a sinful nation and risk their own lives and favor vis-à-vis God. Prayer changes people, and it changes God.

The positive aspect of despair resides in the interrogative mode of address. Loss of optimism forces one to ask questions about long-held verities and to test religious claims against the realities of experience. Wherever anomie, lawlessness, and chaos in general enter the picture, one has to search for guilt, ascribing it either to human beings or to the Deity. Genuine skeptics shy away from attributing blame to humans when radical evil derives from the Creator. Despair therefore keeps us honest. Moreover, such questioning of the tradition grows out of a profound commitment to the vision of a better order, one sustained by the Lord of the universe. In a very real sense, therefore, a skeptic has more faith than the individual who rests comfortably in divine arms without recognizing that religion has become a magical fetish.

My own religious life is sustained by this sense that genuine belief requires constant questioning. For me, the intellect does not have to be sacrificed on the altar of convenience. We have been granted the power to question and to search for truth, and no amount of inquiry poses a threat to the Lord of truth and life. The marvel is that I have not been driven to abandon all belief in Transcendence.

The primary reason for that tenacious adherence to faith is my strong sense of wonder and a feeling that gratitude ought to characterize human beings in such a majestic universe. I am overwhelmed on every side by such mystery that no amount of persuasion could convince me to give up belief in creative intention underlying the world as we encounter it. As a gardener and one who often comes in close contact with the earth, I know that my destiny is to join the earthworms that frequent the soil. Whether that will be my final resting place I cannot say, but the quality of life here and now makes my religious allegiance worthwhile nonetheless. To be sure, one can provide a philosophical base for moral obligation and for an aesthetic sense of wonder apart from religious commitment, but I choose to maintain loyalty to a tradition that has informed my life and that of those persons who have enriched my experiences for nearly sixty years.

If Reinhold Niebuhr is correct in his assessment of the situation, it seems to me that a few persons who see it as their mission in life to advance the interrogative mode of dealing with reality are less of a threat to Christianity than the masses who accept everything without question and at the same time run the risk of failing to appreciate either the agony or the ecstasy of faith.

Be Still, My Heart

The human intellect stands at the door of suffering and its companion, death, without a key. Even those of us who specialize
in assigning reasons for the wholly irrational are silenced by extreme
suffering and the early death of good people. In these instances, none
of the usual explanations suffices. Who can be content with such
feeble responses as these: She suffered to learn patience; she endured
pain so that others might not have to do so; she purified her soul
through the fire of testing. The plain truth is that none of us has a
clue about the mystery of suffering, why it strikes some people with
staggering force and seems to overlook others with virtual neglect.
In my own case, I have found the academic task of writing about
suffering almost routine. Applying theory to a single instance, Elma
Tyler's, is quite another matter. The memory of her beautiful face
personalizes what I say, introducing an element of subjectivity and
a powerful sense of loss. That involvement swells to the breaking
point when I perceive the pain in the faces of those I love.

I shall not cheapen Elma's last years by offering explanations.
No satisfactory ones exist. For my own peace of mind, I shall say
that the Judeo-Christian faith has taken death seriously, incorporat-
ing suffering into the very nature of God. Refusing to believe that
everyone deserves the evil that may befall him or her, religious
thinkers substituted compassionate love for power as the divine
essence, in this way avoiding the charge that a benevolent God
allowed injustice from malice. Suffering belongs to God's very nature,
we believe, so that when we fall into pain's clutches, we have the

potential of participating in the divine pathos. Only in this way can I continue to believe in the existence of a transcendent Being: by believing that when pain engulfed Elma's body, God shed the first tear, and that tear bathes us in love right now.

Such a God understands our anger at the waste represented by Elma's death. So many dreams are shattered with a single blow. Her departure renders shallow the well-known exuberant invitation to grow old along with me, with its promise that the best is yet to be. Not so. Only memory will remain, a poor substitute for her vibrant presence. Our loss is colossal. A mother must say good-bye to one she expected to pre-depart; a sister and a brother must relinquish a lifetime of accessibility; a loving husband must return to an empty house with a million reminders of her absence; four grown children must forever forfeit those animated conversations with a mother who loved them more than life itself; two of them have enlarged the family circle, and thus the circle of sorrow, one that touches me deeply. Co-workers and friends widen the circle still. Yes, our loss is monumental. The universe is not fair, and I shall openly proclaim it in your midst.

That is not my final word, however, for the mystery of life includes joy as well as suffering. Perhaps our capacity for joy is related integrally to our drinking from the cup of sorrow. Elma's memory is best served by celebrating what she was. As I talk about my perception of her, others will, of course, substitute what they saw in her. My own insights came from special occasions in the Tylers' home: a dinner when David and Cynthia's love had become manifest (another in our home to cement that relationship further during their graduation from Vanderbilt); the preparation for and celebration of two weddings — Laurie and Steve's, and Cynthia and David's; two Christmas celebrations (and another meal in our home in Durham). I shall always remember Elma's gracious smile when she welcomed us into her home, her lively wit, her oyster dressing and golden biscuits, her quiet dignity, and the magisterial way she ran a household, momentarily filled with three generations and some outsiders who were made to feel completely at home. I shall remember her skill at charades, her love for the garden, her devotion to the environment and to rational planning of parenthood, her courage in suffering, and her refusal to allow pain to turn her thoughts selfishly within. Elma celebrated life, and we honor her memory when we do the same.

Because Elma has touched us all, we shall never be the same again. As we shed tears over our loss, let us take comfort in the fact that her suffering has ended. Like the ancient Egyptian poet, she could well have said that "death is in my sight today like an infant's reaching for its mother's breast." My religious convictions lead me to add that the One who shaped Elma in her mother's womb and nurtured her for five-and-a-half decades has lifted her in strong arms and borne her into eternity. That same Ancient of Days will dry our tears, collecting them in a precious vessel so that none is lost, and will surround us all with comfort. How else can we explain the many caring people who have reached out in love to help ease our pain? This expression of tenderness is God at work to those who have eyes to see.

Let us pray.

O Thou who art not a stranger to suffering,
whose sorrow encompasses a cross on Calvary,
look with compassion on a stricken family
and begin the process of healing here and now.
For Elma's life, we give thee thanks —
for her love, her beauty, her intelligence.
May those in whose lives she invested her own
find solace in knowing that her spirit remains,
filling us with warmth and gratitude.
Comforter of the discomfited,
grant us thy peace in this hour
and henceforth forevermore.
Amen.

The One Who Takes Life
Can Give It Back

Isaiah 28:21; Luke 24:21

One of the most poignant stories in the Bible makes an extraordinary concession that some of Jesus' close followers had their deepest hopes aroused, only to experience their complete dashing when Roman soldiers silenced an innocent Judean prophet. The recently snuffed flame flickered momentarily when astonishing news reached them that he who had suffered public shame on the Cross was now alive, but cold winds of doubt prevailed — until they met a stranger on the road to their home in Emmaus whose familiarity with the Scriptures and whose behavior rekindled the coals of their hearts and restored hope. Now their despairing "We had hoped" is transformed into an exhilarating "Did not our hearts burn within while he talked with us on the way and opened the scriptures for us?"

We, too, have had our hopes rise and fall. The Bestower of Life performed the greatest miracle of all, evoking in us profound appreciation and anticipation, only to give way to pluperfect despair. "We had hoped for the birth of little ones whom we could hold in our arms and whom we could love for the rest of our lives, but now that hope has expired." How prophetic Isaiah's words: "Strange is his deed; alien is his work!" Grief has overpowered us, because it has touched those we love most fervently. In their loss of hope also rests ours; together we shall walk that lonely road toward the village of Emmaus.

As we walk, however, we shall remember that Jesus did not leave his followers comfortless. In small ways not exactly clear from the story, he instilled renewed hope in disconsolate followers. Death is not the last word, for "the living One" has removed its sting, although not its reality. Jesus reaches out to us and beckons us to put our trust in the One who announces the dawn of God's kingdom in our hearts. Like those followers long ago, we can move from lost hope to the promise of divine presence. Whatever else that signifies, it definitely proclaims life and love. Knowing this, we walk in the shadow of despair until we emerge into the light of life; as we journey on that weary road, we await the kind stranger whose words and deeds renew our hope and awaken our spirit, transforming the "We had hoped" into an imperative "Hope in God," and restoring confidence that no one who hopes in the gracious Father will be disappointed.

PRAYERS

We pray for those who think they are strong but are really weak,
   and for the truly powerful who think they are without strength;
for those who think they are healthy but are actually sick
      to the core,
   and for those who, though riddled with pain,
      possess soundness of mind and heart;
for those who have access to more than their share
      of worldly goods,
   and for those whose only treasure consists of your pleasure;
for those who gather many loved ones into their arms,
   and for the lonely soul who longs to be embraced with love;
for those who bravely face daily temptation,
   and for the ones who cower in fear lest evil prevail;
for those whose hearts are torn with grief,
   and for those who know no feelings at all;
for those who labor to secure their future,
   and for those who perceive the futility of it all;
for those who laugh, dance, and celebrate life's good things,
   and for all who weep over the injustice of cruel reality;
for those in prisons, real or imagined,
   and for all who take their freedom for granted.

We pray, merciful Parent, for this congregation:
replace self-justification and defensiveness with contrition,
remove bitterness and loss of face;
attend our wounds, O great Physician, with Gilead's balm,
purge all impurities with your consuming fire;
clothe us all with the beauty of forgiveness,
and at last teach us your will.
Amen.

Sovereign of the universe, you who dwell in the vast regions of space yet are as near as a whisper, you created us, and you sustain us in your love. We have come to this place because we have an overwhelming sense of gratitude for so many things. We love and are loved; we close our eyes in rest without fear of harm during the night; our pantries are filled with nutritious foodstuffs; we spend our waking hours in pursuits that bring pleasure and profit; we look for ways to help others in need. For us, life is truly good. At the same time, we acknowledge a profound sense of need. Our personal relationships easily become fractured; we fear an unknown harm that threatens us and those we love; we see inequities that leave some people destitute, hungry, and violent; we recognize the tyranny of work and resent its impact on our families; we feel helpless before monumental poverty on a worldwide scale. So we place our lives in your hands, asking only that your will be done. You alone know the extent of our need and our sorrow; you alone can meet our needs and provide rest for the weary. Therefore we adore you for now and forever, and we implore your presence as our hearts beat a mighty rhythm of praise to the source of life. Amen.

O you who dwell beyond reach of the imagination,
   safe from the fallout of our daily holocausts,
dare we ask that you go with us into paths inconsequential
     and shoddy,
   that you bestow holiness upon our godless and
     God-forsaken lives?
Yet do you not precede us to the places where life
    has become death,
   go before us to announce glad tidings that we are free
    to become your children?
Father, enable us babes to follow your ever-enlarging
   footsteps where need is present,
And open our eyes to the sacred in every aching heart. Amen.

O you who dwell beyond reach of the imagination,
   whose gifts to us infinitely surpass our gratitude —
     a university that encourages us to search for the unknown
      without fear of the consequences,
     colleagues who challenge our ideas but befriend us still,
     students whose enthusiasm spills over on us,
     countless others, known and unknown, whose toil
      makes our lives both productive and pleasant.
For these and other tokens of your boundless generosity,
   we are truly thankful. Amen.

Possessor of Infinite Wisdom, before whom full knowledge plays from morning to night, and whose eyes search the hearts of women and men, we invoke your presence and patience upon this celebration of partial insight that these students and their instructors have acquired. We need your presence, because apart from you there can be no understanding, only groping in the darkness of our own selfish ambitions. We must have your forbearance, since our puny truths aspire to greatness but stumble before finitude itself. Together we teachers and students have advanced eagerly to the door of knowledge, at last to be barred from entrance. Unable to fathom the secrets of the universe, we have gazed through the window upon an unspeakable treasure, and have longed to sit down and talk with you for days on end. Until now we have camped outside your dwelling — hoping, longing, waiting for wisdom. Silently, you have listened to our ceaseless babblings. Perhaps, just perhaps, like Job of old we should put our hands to our mouths in the presence of the Eternally Silent One. Perchance the combination of divine and human silence would constitute a veritable dialogue of love, stilling our anxious questions forever. O lover of truth, may we ministers of your wondrous good news settle for nothing less than a dialogue of love. Amen.

Thou Source of Infinite Wisdom,
how clearly we behold the ugly dimensions of reality —
     starving masses,
     religious fanatics who snuff out human life
          as readily as we extinguish a match,
     racial violence,
     greed running rampant in multinational corporations.
If our tired eyes must behold such ugliness day after day,
open them, we pray, to the beauty that also surrounds us —
     the silent trees blushing in anticipation of standing in thy
presence unclothed during the wintry months,
     the excitement of students as they encounter fresh insights,
     the extended hand of a colleague,
     the hope that survives death itself. Amen.

O Ever Silent One, pardon our stammering tongues
    and faltering voices.
But how else can we talk to you when we know our words will
    only echo the silence of eternity?
Our fathers and mothers have taught us to address you as
    'abinu malkenu, our Father, our King,
And we have learned the words so well that they flow
    from our tongues like turbulent waters.
Still, when we pause to consider what we mean by these hallowed
    words, we wish to qualify both, for we are, after all,
      theologians.
How can we call you Father when women feel thereby excluded,
    when millions of your children die of starvation,
And their earthly parents die a thousand deaths watching the
    little bodies waste away?
How can we call you King when cruel greed thrives
    and virtue flags, and your subjects race toward mass suicide?
Like Gideon of old, we demand that you confirm any truth
    in credal affirmation, for we have mastered the art of disbelief.
Our victory has been a Pyrrhic one; lonely men and women
    of faith in a silent universe, we ache to hear your voice
    and to feel the warmth of your hand on ours.
For after all, doesn't a child have that right?
Perchance you are teaching us to extend a hand to one another
    and, by speaking a word of love to our brothers and sisters,
    to shatter bitter loneliness.
Nay, even this formulation assumes that we are strong
    and bestow health on others.
'Abinu malkenu, we who live on borrowed breath concede
    our beggar status before you and your other children.
Touch, we pray, our extended hands, engulf us with your
    eternal silence, and sanctify our voiceless cry!

O Thou whose presence moves the morning stars to sing for joy,
    whose glory the heavens declare without words,
Teach us "peddlers-of-words" the nobility of silence
    so that we may truly know speech's grandeur;
Enable us to pause while listening to others praise thee,
    and mightily to extol thee when they grow silent.
Touch, we pray, our trembling lips and engulf us
      with celestial music,
    fashioning love's lyric from the stammering of our tongues.

God,

Here we go again, nodding in your direction before beginning to work, hoping to secure your approval for all our deliberations. Our thoughts are scattered from here to our latest project; anger mounts because of never-ending nuisances — another faculty meeting, yet another committee assignment, still one more knock at the door — and we necessarily bring all that baggage along and plop it down in front of you. But are things any different with you? Aren't your creatures always making demands upon you? Heal my sick child, give me a new heart, enable us to feed the hungry, and so on. Is that why you are always silent? You don't have time to talk? Perhaps if we didn't bother you so much, and thus lifted part of the load from your shoulders, you could pause long enough to pass the time of day with us. But I am not so sure we would slow down enough to hear you even then. After all, we have important things to do. God help us! Amen.

Fashioner of the Universe, Giver and Sustainer of Life, Source of All Wisdom, we give you thanks for everyone gathered here today, both those persons who have newly decided to become a part of this university and those of us who have been entrusted with decision-making that will shape our future together. Enable us to act wisely and to foster an environment that encourages learning on the part of one and all. Teach us humility even in the presence of exciting discoveries that may ease suffering, lessen prejudice, or broaden horizons of knowledge. Bestow on us all a sense of gratitude for the gift of intelligence and make us thankful for those countless individuals who have made this institution a place where students and faculty unite to learn. Above all else, give us an awareness of our potential to do good — and harm — and sustain us in the struggle against ignorance and indifference. Amen.

O Silent One,
   hidden from vulnerable eyes!
We lift up our voices,
   full of grief for a fallen classmate,
   and we dare to hope you can make sense
   of what to us seems wasteful,
      indeed tragic.
May we examine ourselves anew
   as a result of Eugene's death,
   ever alert to conquer the forces
   that fracture relationships
   both human and divine. Amen.

Conclusion

The office of ministry has lost something of its luster in the eyes of twentieth-century Americans. No longer is the minister one of the most educated persons in the community, a person whose wide reading and mastery of the classics empowered him — the masculine pronoun is intentional — to speak authoritatively within society and to command a hearing. Today's church officials, rightly or wrongly, seldom seem to consider intellectual acumen as the *sine qua non* of ordination, and theological education has become narrowly specialized like other professions such as law and medicine. In such a situation it is gratifying to see how many learned persons, many after successful careers, choose to enter the ministry and to devote their lives to a profession that, with few exceptions, offers meager material rewards.

This willingness to enter a life of service is all the more surprising when one ponders the difficulty of functioning as spokesperson for another, especially one whose very existence is denied by a large segment of society. Years ago during my days as a pastor I quickly discovered the agony of indecision arising from a lack of any definite way of determining exactly what God wanted me to say to a congregation awaiting moral leadership. After hours of struggling to choose a topic for the weekly sermon, I had no assurance that the final selection and its exposition corresponded to divine will. In my own experience, and I suspect the same is true for others as well, speaking on behalf of God was first and foremost a "literary conceit," one carried on humbly and with no intent to deceive.

Sadly, the ministry attracts a few unworthy persons whose arrogance leads them to claim that their own words actually coincide in every respect with those of the One for whom they are expected to speak. This presumption of office brings infamy to a profession already suffering from societal indifference. A few dishonorable ministers, often in the public eye through the media of television, seem intent on personal aggrandizement at anyone's expense. Their moral bankruptcy only lowers the status of the ministry in the eyes of the public, and as a result many good people suffer for the sins of a few. The claims of power-hungry television evangelists to communicate God's will must be exposed for what they are, outright lies, pious language about the holy spirit notwithstanding. Their blasphemous pretense of intimate contact with God suggests that the conceit of the sermon has a negative sense.

A second sense of sermonic conceit lacks such negative connotations. I refer to the resemblance between prophetic proclamation in the Bible and a minister's proclamation of the gospel. Ancient prophets purported to speak divine words, as indeed do modern ministers. Men and women like Isaiah, Amos, and Huldah availed themselves of formulas such as "Thus hath Yahweh spoken" and "Whisper of Yahweh," both of which suggested that what followed derived from God in every detail. On examination, however, this literary fiction hardly carries such heavy baggage. The move from divine revelation to proclaimed speech included quite a number of steps.

The following process best describes that move from initial revelatory experience to prophetic proclamation: (1) consciousness that a dark, enigmatic word or vision was sent by God; (2) contemplation of the meaning of this revelation; (3) a poetic phrasing of the message; (4) the addition of reinforcing grounds, threats, and motivation; (5) the articulation of that message in the light of tradition; and (6) the actual delivery of the prophetic word, accompanied by rhetorical flourish and gestures. The human contribution to the revelatory process was absolutely essential, so that in the end divine and human words merged into one. At times the prophet was not even certain that the final message resulting from this arduous intellectual process had not suppressed the original revelation altogether, as an incident in

Jeremiah's ministry reveals. Confronted by a conflicting prophetic word confidently proclaimed by the prophet Hananiah, a confused Jeremiah was reduced to silence for the moment — although not forever, as the subsequent narrative makes clear.

The sermons in this book give voice to my own understandings of reality. That much is certain. They make no claim to derive from God. Still, I have honestly and attentively listened to the biblical text, hoping to discover in it a voice that has been silent for as long as I can recall. My goal has been to recover that voice, if only as an echo, and to translate it into contemporary religious language. I have meditated deeply about vexing theological problems, and I have tried to give voice to my deepest spiritual longings. For one in my religious tradition, written prayers require justification, at least in many congregations. I assume that a minister can be spontaneous in the study just as readily as one can in the pulpit, and I truly believe that the Creator honors articulate speech above inarticulate speech. Moreover, in my view, prayer's importance demands that ministers devote time to it commensurate with its significance to the religious life.

The majority of sermons and meditations in this collection take their point of departure in the Old Testament. That fact should surprise no one who knows anything about my teaching responsibilities. The choice of Old Testament texts arises from my deep conviction that the One to whom the Torah, prophets, and writings bear witness is the same One whom gospel, epistle, and apocalypse attest. My decision to emphasize the Old Testament springs from my belief that ministers neglect this body of literature to their peril, for no one can understand the New Testament without knowing the religious traditions that gave it shape.

If my efforts at taking the Bible seriously and submitting to its witness strike responsive chords in readers, I shall consider my time well spent. If the sermons, meditations, and prayers in this book elicit among readers a single reaction, a trembling at the threshold of a biblical text, such extraordinary burning within the heart bears witness to the One in whose name all three are written and about whom a story of monumental proportions has sprung up among astonished witnesses.